PERSPECTIVES IN TEACHER EDUCATION

About the Author

G.N. Prakash Srivastava, a senior faculty in NCERT at Regional Institute of Education, Bhubaneswar has a number of books and national as well as regional projects to his credit, including 'Recent Trends in Educational Psychology', 'Recent Approaches to Personality study', 'Personality and Academic Prediction', 'Advanced Research Methodology', 'Aadhunik Shiksha Manovigyan', 'Vikas Manovigyan Evam Shiksha', 'Shiksha Manovigyan', 'Navin Vichardharaein', and 'Management of Teacher Education'. Also, he is co-author of 'Child Understanding and Development, Handbook of Social Teaching' (NCERT), and 'Indian Girls'. More than 80 papers and 15 monographs, 5 MHRD Projects and ERIC (NCERT) Project on 'Restructuring Internship in Teaching' are also his significant contributions. His MHRD, Govt. of India sponsored deputation to Israel brought forth an important report on the 'Education of Gifted Children'. As coordinator he has published "Teacher Education for Value Inculcation" a report of NCERT sponsored National Seminar, and "Nurturing Values Through School Education" the report of (NCERT) Regional Seminar. His name has been included in "Learned Asia", "Indo-European: Who's Who," "Who's Who in Indo-American Education", and "Reference Asia: Who's who of Men and Women of Achievement". The American Biographical Institute (ABI), U.S.A. selected him for the decree of "Man of the Year, 1998," Who's who of the year 1999," "2000 Millennium Medal of Honor", and "Outstanding Man of the 20th century."

He has submitted his thesis for D. Litt. in Education on 'Present Scenario and Perspective Model of Teacher Training in India'.

PERSPECTIVES IN TEACHER EDUCATION

G.N. PRAKASH SRIVASTAVA

Professor, Department of Education
Regional Institute of Education (NCERT),
Bhubaneswar, Orissa

CONCEPT PUBLISHING COMPANY, NEW DELHI-110059

ISBN 81-8069-088-1 (PB)

First Published 2004

Published and Printed by
Ashok Kumar Mittal
Concept Publishing Company
A/15-16, Commercial Block, Mohan Garden
New Delhi- 110059 (India)

Phones : 25351460, 25351794
Fax : 091-(11) - 25357103
Email : publishing@conceptpub.com

PREFACE

The central theme of Teacher Education is teacher preparation. The development of the normal school in the early 19th century included the apprenticeship approach in the teacher education curriculum. The "Practice Teaching" concept lingered on for many years, through the Teacher Colleges era into schools of education in multipurpose institutions. The philosophy persisted until middle of the twentieth century in the advanced countries and then the "Practice Teaching" gave way to "Student Teaching" in which the prospective teacher was considered to be student of teaching during the classroom experience.

As a vehicle for teacher education and certification, the "Internship" can be traced to the early years of the present country, although many persons are inclined to consider the "Internship" in teacher education as a significant departure in teacher preparation. Milestones in the development of the "Internship" concept of the Brown University Programme which began in 1909, the Co-operative Programme of the University of Cincinnati and Cincinnati Public Schools in 1919, the expansion of Internship Programme of 1930s, and the importance provided to it in 1950s, and 1960s. In spite of this fairly long historical background, however, the Internship has yet to become a significant factor in the mass production of teachers.

The term "Internship" refers to an arrangement under which a prospective teacher can acquire first hand experience as a teacher in situations closely resembling those in which he/she would be working upon entering the profession. Regional Colleges/Institutes of Education as constituent units of NCERT have been organising Internship in Teaching Programme since their inception where as other institutions of teacher-training have been using the terms "Practice Teaching" of "Teaching Practice" or so. Secondary

Teacher Education Curriculum (NCERT, 1991) has coined a new term "School Experience Programme (SEP) in place of Internship in Teaching. With the passage of time a number of researches and innovations in the field of teacher-training have brought many approaches, methods, strategies and designs in this field. The need for the present document was felt due to deterioration in the Teacher Preparation Programme. It provides a prospective model of Teacher Education.

I am thankful to Prof. J. S. Rajput, Director NCERT who has always been a source of inspiration, motivation and guidance in my academic ventures, Prof. P. K. Khanna for the encouragement provided by him, and Shri A. C. Pachauri for his scholarly feedback and encouragement to all my academic works. I acknowledge with gratitude the contribution of Prof. Dwight W. Allen, Prof. S. N. Tripathi, and Dr. S. S. Srivastava. My thanks are also due to all the Teacher Educators, Co-operating School Principals/Teachers and Interns of the various parts of the country who shared their views for restructuring Teacher Education.

I place on record my gratefulness to my colleague Dr. Iqbal Ahamed for his help and suggestions in the completion of the work. The assistance provided by Mr. Arun Gupta, Ajay Publishers and Distributors, Bhopal and Mr. Suhas Chaudhari, Dynamic Computers Bhopal cannot be forgotten. I am thankful to them.

I hope the book will provide new dimensions to teacher education and directions to teacher training in the third millennium.

Bhubaneswar G. N. PRAKASH SRIVASTAVA
Ist October, 2003

CONTENTS

1

INTRODUCTION

"Teaching is a system of actions intended to produce learning". Learning is often defined as a "Relatively permanent change in behaviour". Clarke (1770) defines teaching as "activities that are designed and performed to produce change in student (pupil)". The Educative Teaching has been considered as a practice which engages the rational faculties of students and respects them as independent centres of thought and action supported by evidence, developing the power of students to gather the evidence by most reliable methods for discovering the truth and to make students intelligent and reflective in the exercise of their skills.

Teaching has been taken as training, conditioning and indoctrination. The generic concept of teaching considers it as action undertaken to bring about learning. It is not only telling but it is face to face encounter contributing to learning or bringing change in the learning behaviour of the student. Teaching includes explaining, describing, demonstrating, exemplifying, guiding, lecturing, defining, rating, appraising, interpreting, questioning, elaborating, indentifying, designating, comparing and the like activities.

Teaching is behaving in a social context and is therefore amenable to scientific observation and analysis. Teaching behaviour is modifiable by feeding back to the student teacher (pupil teacher or teacher trainee) about his on-going behaviour in the classroom and the result of his teaching in terms of the children's behaviour in learning.

Desired behaviour in the student is rewarded to ensure its persistence, a practice that is explicable with reference to learning theory. Similarly, the student teacher's teaching is understandable and controllable only in terms of theories of teaching. The five major areas in which contributions have been made to the theory of teaching need only be briefly mentioned here.

Firstly, Educational goals and objectives have received wide attention and study. Empirical data and logical reasoning have led to the drawing up to taxonomies of educational objectives in the cognitive and affective areas (Bloom, *et al*; 1956, and Krathwohl *et al.* 1964). These have led to the preparation of detailed objectives suitable for classroom fulfillment and to a methodology for the preparation of objectives suitable for use by practising teachers and students (Mager, 1962).

Secondly, the teachers and pupil's verbal behaviour in the classroom has been observed and analysed. The interaction between the teachers and pupils verbal behaviour has been studied and this behaviour has been related on the pupil's learning (Medley and Mitzel 1963a, b; Bellack *et al*; 1966, Flanders, 1961).

Thirdly, techniques and strategies for producing cognitive growth in pupils have been evolved and presented for teacher's use (Taba, 1965).

Fourthly, Classroom and group management has received detailed empirical study and a body of theoretical and practical knowledge has been amassed which began to put the problem of discipline on a scientific footing (Kounin, 1970).

Lastly, Teacher's personality traits and their relation to both teacher's and pupil's behaviour had been an object of considerable research (Getzels and Jackson, 1963; Ryans, 1960).

Teaching is a complex activity. For its accomplishment one requires a certain amount of knowledge, understanding and expertise in various teaching skills. The whole activity of classroom teaching can be divided into two phases, viz, interactive phase and non-interactive phase. Non-interactive phase can further be sub-divided in two stages: i.e., pre-interactive and post-interactive stages. The pre-interactive stage involves planning and preparation for the interactive stage. This stage is generally utilised for lesson planning, collecting and preparing teaching aids, preparing assignments etc. The post-interactive stage involves analysis of what has been done in the interactive stage.

In the interactive phase teacher has a face to face interaction with his pupils. The interactive phase should result in the desired changes in the behaviour of the student as well as of the teacher. Before imparting instruction the teacher should have a clear idea about the existing knowledge level of the student. He should be aware of the environmental influences acting on the mind of the students at the time of teaching. The teacher should know how he can best attract the attention of the pupils and how that attention can be retained throughout. He should be skilled enough to arouse curiosity and interest of the pupil, forward the topic and invite their maximum involvement in the teaching learning process. There are many such challenges for a person entering the profession of teaching which led to Teacher-Training, Practice Teaching and Internship in Teaching.

1.1 Teacher Training

Practice Teaching and Internship : In Retrospect

The development of the normal school in the early 19th century included the apprenticeship approach in the teacher education curriculum. The approach was largely that of "Practising" the teacher acts. The "Practice Teaching" concept lingered for many years, through the teacher's college era into schools of education in multipurpose institutions. Practice teaching was based on the premise that the prospective teacher was first taught the theory and then introduced to the classroom teaching to practice that theory.

The philosophy persisted until the middle of twentieth century in the advanced countries and then the practice teaching approach changed along with terminology of the experience. "Practice Teaching" gave way to "Student Training" in which the prospective teacher was considered to be a student of teaching during the classroom experience. The changed philosophy resulted from the realization that teachers could not be educated away from the realities of the classroom and that theory could be assimilated only as it was put into action. Thus theory was related to teaching and learning in a more meaningful way. With proper help and guidance from the supervisory personnel who would work with him the student teacher would expand and develop his understanding of teaching.

The position of "Cooperating Teacher" gave the teacher opportunity to ply his trade—another opportunity to teach. The use of video cameras enabled the student teacher to see himself at work in the classroom, and the addition of interaction analysis techniques made it possible to quantify the process of teaching into the identifiable categories. The entire supervisory process rapidly became more analytical in its approach.

It became obvious that if he were to attain the new goals of student teaching, the prospective teacher required a longer, more varied, and more extensive classroom experience. This led to the move from the college campus to the public schools, where longer assignments were possible.

As currently used the term "teaching practice" has three major connotations : the practicing of teaching skills and acquisition of the role of a teacher; the whole range of experience that students go through in schools; and the practical aspects of the course as distinct from theoretical studies.

1.2 Objectives of Student Teaching/Practice Teaching

The shift toward the more analytical approach to student teaching has resulted in a change in objectives. No longer is student teaching expected to result in mere tricks of the trade; the objectives are more global in nature. Hillard and Durrance (1968) and Brimer and Cope (1971) listed the objectives of student teaching as under :

The student teaching experience, if it occurs in a clinical climate, does provide valuable means for guiding the student teacher's growth through a carefully planned sequence of activities which enable him to :

- Clarify his understanding of the purposes, dvelopment, programmes, and administrative organization of education.

- Broaden his understanding of curricular practices.
- Become sensitive to the social patterns of a school community and discover through first hand experiences ways of improving curriculum for pupils by effective use of community resources.
- Develop wholesome professional attitudes toward members of the teaching profession.
- Identify his strong points and weak points in the wide spectrum of competencies associated with effective teaching.
- Become increasingly resourceful and creative in planning, developing, and evaluating effective learning experience for and with pupils.

The Indiana University statement suggests that the student teaching experience should attempt :

- To provide for professional development of young teachers through integration of theory and practice.
- To promote the growth of student-teachers by encouraging them to read and to become familiar with professional books, magazines, resource units, audio-visual aids, and other materials related to their teaching experiences.
- To develop certain important abilities involved in planning teaching-learning activities; in organising materials of instruction to provide for the individual needs, interests and capacities of youth; in handling routine elements of classroom management; and in evaluating pupil's, educational growth
- To continue the development of essential personality characteristics of teachers such as breadth of interest, curiosity, dependability, and co-operation.
- To provide the student teacher with an opportunity for applying theory to be applied in the practical situation and to assist him, where necessary, to discriminate between inappropriate theory and the inadequate implementing of sound theory.

- To provide the student with an experience of success in the teaching situation so that the student acquires confidence.
- To provide an opportunity in the practical teaching situations for the extension and deepening of the student-teachers self-knowledge.
- To provide the student with practical experience in schools which will reveal some of the problems of discipline and enable him to develop personal methods of control.
- To provide the student with an opportunity of becoming part of the school community, familarizing himself with its practices and entering into appropriate professional relationships with its adult members, the most significant of which is his relationship with the class or subject teacher.
- To provide for the interchange of ideas and methods between schools and college by college staff and students perceiving new ideas, materials and equipment in use in schools, and by college staff and students introducing new ideas, materials and equipment into schools.

Perhaps the most important outcome for student teaching is a personal one—the development of self-confidence and a sense of security to the point where he can enter his first teaching position with a feeling of competence. This self-confidence is the result of the many varied activities in which the student teacher participates in the well-planned and well-developed practice teaching programme.

1.3 The Context of Practice Teaching

Aspects of practice teaching other than the pedagogical have been subject to investigation and analogous comments made on its essentially conservative nature. Students are concerned to present a favourable image to the schools and the training institution as a way of surviving practice teaching so that they are anxious to conform to what they perceive to be the expectations of their supervisors. This impression management frequently results in students engaging in activities not because of any conviction that they are intrinsically desirable but because they are expected to impress the supervisor. Practice teaching should aim to change this state of affairs and develop in students a habit of scepticism and enquiry not just in regard to pedagogical practices but also in their appraisal of the institutions in which they teach.

1.4 Assessment of Practice Teaching

The assessment of practice teaching for the purposes of certification is a very problematic subject. To a great extent this is a consequence of the apprenticeship approach. Student teachers have inevitably been graded according to the criteria held by individual teachers or specific institutions and the criteria have not always been made explicit (Stones and Morris, 1972). For example, teachers have been assessed according to the degree that their personalities resembled those of the adjudicating headteachers (Wiseman and Start, 1965); idiosyncratically according to the institution they happened to be training in (Stones and Morris, 1972); and on vague conceptions of what was being judged (McCulloch, 1979).

In attempts to introduce a degree of rigour and objectivity into the assessment of practice teaching, schedules have been produced by many teacher training institutions. These schedules itemize those aspects of teaching performance thought to be critical in satisfactory teaching. Student teachers are awarded marks on a scale for each aspect by supervisors or co-operating teachers. Examples of items from schedules are : "Clarity of aims; pacing of the lesson—skill in explaining and narrating; quality of voice and speech habits; presentation advanced with appropriate pace and timing; voice clear, attractive, and well-modulated; blackboard well-used; lesson method suitable". The first two are taken from a widely used American schedule, the second pair from a British schedule, the third pair from an Australian instrument, and the fourth from a teacher assessment form used in schools in the United Kingdom in the nineteenth century which gives an indication of the rate of change in this approach.

While the devising of check lists against which to evaluate student teaching is a move towards objectifying the process of assessment, scrutiny of the schedules available reveals some problems. Although the various schedules have a certain degree of similarity, they are, in fact, all different. Their discrepant nature illustrates the lack of clarity and consensus on the nature of the desirable criteria of practical teaching. Further, the awarding of marks on a scale for each item on the schedule is in most cases extraordinarily difficult and depends a great deal on the assessors' ideas and values. It is possible, by systematic training, to get assessors to grade student teachers similarly, that is, award them roughly the same marks on each item of the schedule thus producing marker consistency. However the fact that markers are consistent does not necessarily guarantee that the teaching has been effective.

Many of the schedules pay little attention to children's learning. Stones and Morris (1972) in a survey of all training institutions in England, Wales, and Northern Ireland found that hardly any assessors of practice teaching assessed their students on the criterion of whether the pupils they were trying to teach learned anything or not. As the examples taken from the schedules suggest the focus is on what the student teacher does and there is an implicit inference that the activity under scrutiny will produce children's learning. A moment's reflection will indicate that this inference is not necessarily justified. Clear, well-modulated, and attractive voices will not teach children very much of worth if what the teacher is saying is nonsense. Much the same could be said about other teacher characteristics that form part of many assessment schedules.

Thus although the devising of schedules for the assessment of teaching has the merit of making explicit the criteria to be considered, there is little evidence so far that the actual items on the schedules are likely to enable assessors to make more valid judgments of students if pupil learning is taken to be the crucial cirterion of teacher competence as in logic it should be. But even if attention is paid to pupil learning there is a further difficult problem. Current methods of assessing pupil learning are themselves far from perfect. Student teachers are very rarely equipped by their training to make sensitive and valid assessment of their pupils' learning as it relates to the objectives they set themselves at the beginning of their teaching. In many cases student teachers have to make use of published tests that may or may not be appropriate to their own teaching and certainly cannot be geared to their own objectives.

Apart from these considerations, tests very frequently give information about learning only at the verbal level. All too often they depend on memorization and provide little evidence of understanding or competence beyond that of regurgitating what has previously been memorized. Thus any attempt to focus on pupil learning in the assessment of student teaching needs to be viewed with caution even though the attempt should be applauded. Unless the pupils' learning is learning with understanding there is a danger that the assessments of the students will be based on their ability to drill pupils in rote learning as their nineteenth-century predecessors did.

1.5 Possible Perspectives

Many of the problems of practice teaching discussed above spring from a lack of a systematic attempt to teach pedagogy that could unite theoretical studies and practical teaching. Present course organization with the clearly demarcated practice teaching attachments to schools, organized and conducted in separate compartments from theoretical studies, signal to students that the two activities are distinct and preserve the archetypical conception of student teaching as apprentice training.

Pedagogical studies bring together theoretical ideas about the nature of teaching and the processes of human learning because they are task oriented and not merely concerned with the transmission of information. The tasks addressed are two-fold: there is the task the learner faces, that of acquiring new concepts, skills, and understandings; and there is the task the teacher faces, that of so arranging the learning environment of the pupils that they will acquire those skills, concepts, and understandings in a meaningful rather than superficial way. In order to accomplish these tasks the student teacher does not attempt to copy an experienced teacher but draws on a body of knowledge based on research in the fields of human learning and instruction and attempts to implement the appropriate principles in his/her own way according to the circumstances existing at the time.

Practice teaching of this type changes the central concerns of teaching from developing ways of transmitting verbal material to the identification, analysis, and attempted solution of problems of learning and teaching. The student attempts to acquire teaching skills of general application based on principles of teaching and learning. It involves students in attempting to solve pedagogical problems with the assistance of tutors and co-operating teachers. Their job is to help the student teachers to implement the principles effectively and to provide guidance and feedback so that the students' solving, in whole or in part, a variety of teaching problems will help them to build up a body of pedagogical expertise that will be useful to them in a variety of circumstances, but at the same time will be expressed in their own styles and through their own personalities.

Similarly, the preservation of the personal integrity of the student, while operating with a body of principles, can be achieved by the organisation of practice teaching that aims to help students adopt an enquiring approach to the social and educational context of their teaching and to ensure that they are not passively assimilated into a conservative educational milieu. Many writers argue that this is the most important consideration of all in teacher education and some have suggested forms of practice teaching that involve students in making systematic ethnographic studies of the institutions they are practising in, using various observational techniques and methods of analysis so that they can get a deeper understanding of the contextual constraints and opportunities present (Zeichner and Teitelbaum, 1982). Students will thus be enabled to appraise the pedagogical aims set by the school in the light of explicit value positions. They will also obtain insight into the nature of the social forces within institutions that may constrain them in the type of pedagogical activities they might wish to engage in. Students will understand that the nature of schools as they are at present is not part of the natural order of things any more that the various types of teaching they see in the schools are definitive and unchallengable models.

Ethnographic studies and pedagogical studies complement each other. The former give students insights into the desirable aims of and approaches to teaching, and the latter provide insights into the most effective ways of attaining those aims. Together they present a radical reappraisal of traditional practice teaching, but given current questioning of the way things are now, it is possible that some movement towards incorporating some of the ideas will be made in some teacher education programmes in the not too distant future.

1.6 The Future of Practice Teaching

Any future changes should help students develop theory-based practical teaching skills by studying the theory and practice of teaching together just as they would in learning any other subject with a practical component, going from one activity to the other when appropriate the same applies to their ethnographic studies. These should not be regarded as work additional to teaching practice, but an integral part of it. As with pedagogical studies they should be integrated with seminars and study groups within the training institutions as well as within the schools.

A consequence of such approaches would be that the conventional structure of practical teaching experience would change. Instead of student teachers spending an extended period of time briefly observing and then acting as surrogate teachers with similar teaching contact time to that of the other teachers in their practice schools, they will spend much more time in reflecting upon their teaching, in discussing it with others, in planning, and in systematic observation of their practice schools. This type of school experience will help students to obtain an insight into the nature of teaching in its social and educational context and to develop pedagogical skills that spring from an understanding of a body of pedagogical theory rather than rule of thumb or adhoc survival techniques.

It is, therefore, likely that the future organization of many teacher training courses will be much more fluid with students moving between practical activity and learning about pedagogical theory and practice, and the principles and practice of ethnographic enquiry into schools as institutions. Much of this enquiry could take place in school but the actual time devoted to the practical activity of teaching will be reduced and replaced with the reflective activities so lacking at present. The long block of teaching experience in one school with the student acting as surrogate teacher will disappear but the practice teaching that replaces it will be much more informed and effective.

1.7 Internship

Internship is an integral part of professional preparation of a teacher in making preceded by successful observation, participation and student teaching or equivalent clinical experiences in a school environment, and is planned and co-ordinated by the teacher education institution in co-operation with one or more school systems. Intern is a prospective teacher who assumes an internship position in which he is given a teaching position under guidance. Often he is involved in accompanying professional courses simultaneously with his teaching duties.

Internship is service in preparation for a position usually under the supervision of a university or college supervisor and a practicing school teacher more experienced in the field. It consists of wide variety of experiences undertaken in one or more schools. The Intern is given opportunity to participate in many phases of the work of the school system. Frequently his practical work in the school system is correlated with further work at, and or guided by the teacher training institution.

1.8 In Indian Context

Internship in teaching as visualised in the Plan and Programme (NCERT 1963) for which an alternative terminology "School Experience Programme" (SEP) has also been used by Secondary Teacher Education Curriculum (NCERT, 1991) is to be designed to provide opportunities to develop high level of competence in all aspects of the teacher's work. During this period, the student teachers have to work full time in the cooperating schools. They are to be provided with a wide variety of experiences, designed to develop teaching competency such as working with individual students, guiding students, group practice teaching and evaluating students' progress. This has also to provide trainees ample opportunities to acquaint themselves with the school and community and the usual functions of a school. The duties and responsibilities of the teacher of today take him beyond the limits of the class work. Classroom teaching skill is not the only requirement of a good and effective teacher. The teacher training colleges have also to provide experiences in the co-curricular activities, effective library service, organisation of physical games and sports, guidance in choice of courses and careers, reporting students progress, maintenance of record and registers and even aspects like planning for purchase of equipment and apparatus for the laboratory. All these require training and experience for professional efficiency as a teacher. Internship in teaching has to provide the student-teacher an opportunity to acquire all necessary skills for the profession.

1.9 Recent Trends in Preservice Teacher Preparation Programmes

The large scope of policy activity regarding teacher education has led to greater diversity in programme structures. There are a variety of field experiences for candidates. Generally candidates in most secondary teacher education programmes are required to go through some kind of observational and tutorial field experiences prior to student teaching (American Association of Colleges for Teacher Education, 1987). Often during the initial phases of the programme, students spend one or two days per week observing or tutoring in schools. In over two-thirds of the teacher education programmes, field experiences are also required in one or more methods courses later in the programme's sequence. Such experiences allow candidates to apply what they are learning through classroom observations and work with students before entering an intensive student teaching experience (American Association of Colleges for Teacher Education, 1987).

Building on these field experiences, all candidates are involved in practice teaching (also called student teaching), which takes place near the completion of a preparation programme, and occurs in elementary and secondary schools under the supervision of a co-operating teacher. Sometimes, student teaching engages students in two different placements, so that they can experience varied classrooms.

Over the past decade, many schools of education have made great strides in incorporating new understandings of teaching and learning in their curriculum for prospective teachers. More attention to learning theory, cognition, and learning strategies has accompanied a deepening appreciation for content pedagogy and constructivist teaching strategies. In addition, teacher preparation and teacher induction programmes are increasingly introducing strategies that help teachers develop a reflective and problem-solving orientation. This is done by engaging prospective teachers and interns in teacher research, in school-based inquiry, and in learning about students' experiences so that they are building an empirical understanding of learners and a capacity to analyse and reflect on their practice.

In addition to preparation that is rigorous and relevant to today's educational needs, teacher education programmes are increasingly seeking to offer prospective teachers opportunities to work with effective guidance in diverse settings and underserved areas.

An important part of the current redesign of teacher preparation includes efforts to extend the concept of mentoring in more systematic ways within restructured school settings, especially in urban areas. A growing number of education schools are working with school systems to create institutions like professional development schools and internship sites that will allow new teachers to be inducted into schools as they must become, not only schools as they are.

The conditions for thoughtful, adeptive teaching must be well supported by expert, experienced staff in order to be emulated by and instilled in beginning teachers. Because the development of learner-centred practice is enormously difficult, untutored novices often fail at their early attempts. The application of knowledge about learning, teaching, curriculum-building, development, motivation, and behaviour to the individual needs of diverse students is a daunting task requiring skillful observation, diagnosis, and integration of many different concepts and abilities. Unless this occurs with the support of an able mentor, the effort can quickly become overwhelming. This is one of the reasons that knowledge acquired in preservice courses is often not put to use and that beginning teachers' practices often become less sensitive to students' needs rather than more so over the course of their initial year in teaching.

Beginning teachers must develop the ability to apply knowledge appropriately in different contexts while handling the dozens of cognitive, psychological, moral and interpersonal demands that simultaneously require attention in a classroom. Learning to manage the different personalities and needs of twenty-five or thirty children while prioritizing and juggling often conflicting goals does not happen quickly, automatically, or easily. These are skills that have to be developed. Clinical experiences a must enable teachers to learn firsthand about the variability in students' cognitive development and approaches to learning while they are supported with guided instruction and opportunities for reflection on their teaching and its effects on learners. These educative compliments to classroom work should assist novices in acquiring wider repertoires of teaching strategies and help them relate problems of teaching practice to research on teaching and human development. Having these kinds of opportunities available should encourage beginners to teach reflectively, to evaluate what they are doing, to assess whether it is working and why, to understand how to make better decisions, and to juggle the many concerns of teaching.

A growing number of teacher educators have argued that professional development schools may be the best hope for addressing beginning teacher's needs. Like teaching hospitals in the medical profession, they may be structured to provide an environment in which new teachers are gradually introduced to the responsibilities of teaching and are given assistance from experienced colleagues as well as their university-based teachers.

In such environments, beginning teachers receive on-going evaluation and feedback from other teachers about their teaching as well as more formal learning opportunities that enable them to link theory and practice. During a formalized internship or induction year, beginning teachers have opportunities for professional development that encourage collaboration and provide the support that is associated with stronger beginning teacher commitment and efficacy.

Probably the most important recognition of these various teacher education reforms is that prospective teachers must be taught in the same ways in which they will be expected to teach. Like their students must do, teachers also construct their own understandings by doing: collaborating, inquiring into problems, trying and testing ideas, evaluating and reflecting on the outcomes of their work. As teacher educators, beginning teachers, and experienced teachers work together on real problems of practice in learner-centered settings, their development promotes deep understanding that cannot be obtained in coursework alone, although the foundation may be laid in coursework that provides a broader, theoretical frame for developing and interpreting practice.

In the ten-year period between 1976 and 1986, five major proposals for reform for teacher education were published : Educating a Profession (Howsam, Corrigan, Denmark, and Nash, 1976), A Design for a School of Pedagogy (Smith, 1980), "The Phoenix Agenda" (Joyce and Clift, 1984), Tomorrow's Teachers (Holmes Group, 1986), and A Nation Prepared: Teachers for the 21st Century (Carnegie Forum on Education and the Economy, 1986). Each addressed a wide array of issues and problems associated with teacher education and each proposal had as its central reform the call for extending the time spent in teacher preparation.

In India, Secondary Teacher Education Curriculum : A Framework (NCERT, 1991), Programme for Improvement of Secondary Teacher Education Institutions (EDCIL, 1987), and National Policy on Education (MHRD, Government of India, 1986), Curriculum Framework for Teacher Education (NCTE, 1998) are the documents which have provided guidelines to teacher education including teacher training. Establishment of IASEs (Institutes of

Advance Study in Education) and CTEs (Colleges of Teacher Education) were the recent efforts undertaken in the field of Secondary Teacher Education curriculum and training.

In India the past few years have witnessed unprecedented nationwide discussions and debates on education to 'National Reconstruction'. This has culminated in adopting a New Education Policy (National Policy on Education, 1986, 1992) which attached paramount importance to teachers' status and training. But in the absence of specific, self-explanatory objectives of various types of teacher-education programme, we have not gone much beyond changing the titles of the contents of the studies prescribed. The attainment of the teacher is to be assessed in relation to the objectives and the very competence he has acquired during the training. The regional imbalance, and poor relationship between demand and supply of trained teachers due to ill-planned growth of teacher education institution have added to the lowering of standards of teacher education and training. Looking at the National Policy on Education (1986, 1992) the establishment of National System of Education in the country, national core curriculum, achievement of minimum levels of learning by pupils, equality to all in access and success, inculcation of national values in the entire system of education, substantial changes in the content and process of education are some of the parameters envisaged in the policy. The Programme of Action (POA, 1986) for implementation of the National Policy on Education emphasised need for upgradation of quality of secondary teacher education.

The Government of India has made great strides in improving the quality of the teaching corps- raising the pre-service general education requirements, improving pre-service and in-service training, and increasing the number of female teachers and teachers who share their students' social backgrounds. But the capacity of the teaching force to deliver high quality education is constrained by historical deficiencies in teachers' education and training and the absence of performance incentives. As a result, many teachers often have little understanding of the material they teach, possess few teaching skills and are poorly motivated. Thus, to increase the effectiveness of the teaching force the challenge for the next decade is to improve the preparation, motivation, and deployment of teachers (World Bank, 1997).

The preparation of good teachers rests upon the specialization of the subjects or fields to be taught, the professional knowledge and skills and understanding of educational process and teaching skills. In order to keep pace with the changing times, various theories of learning, techniques of instruction, psychological principles of learning and teaching, psychology of learners, experiments and researches in learning and teaching, class and school management, administration of school, problems of adjustment and discipline, current issues like population education, non-formal education, adult education and trends in education — all these have to be included in the broader framework of teacher-education and training.

2

RELATED LITERATURE

The review of related literature shows that numerous studies have been conducted abroad on the various aspects of teacher-training *viz.*, technical skills of teaching, induction of beginning teacher, supervision of practicum, co-operating teachers' perspectives on student teaching, mentoring, and the changing context of teacher education etc. In India, some scattered studies have been conducted and are available on various aspects of teacher preparation. The available studies conducted on teacher training have been presented in this chapter under the following sub-headings :

2.1 Technical Skills of Teaching.
2.2 Supervision of Practicum.
2.3 Induction of Beginning Teachers.
2.4 Mentoring.
2.5 Indian Studies.
2.6 The Changing Context of Teacher Education.

2.1 Technical Skills of Teaching

Technical skills of teaching are specific aspects of teaching behaviour that are considered to be particularly effective in facilitating desired learning in students. The concept of specific teaching skills seems first to have been implemented in teacher education in the micro-teaching programme at Stanford University in the early 1960s. With the subsequent widespread acceptance of micro-teaching as a technique for training teachers, the concept of technical skills of teaching became well-known. In time the concept became an important component of competency-based teacher education and even of competency-based teacher certification (Coker *et al.* 1980).

According to Allen and Ryan (1969) the first technical skill used in the micro-teaching clinic at Stanford University was "how to begin a lesson". Subsequently such skills as achieving "closure", providing "frame of reference", and probing student responses were added until a list was developed which included the following skills:

(a) *Stimulus variation* : using stimulating material and variations in movement, gestures, interaction techniques, and sensory channels in order to alleviate boredom and inattentiveness.

(b) *Set induction* : preparing students for a lesson by clarifying its goals, relating it to students' prior knowledge and skills, through using analogies, demonstrations, and posing stimulating problems.

(c) *Closure* : assisting students to establish links between new and past knowledge by reviewing and applying material to familiar and new examples, cases, and situations.

(d) *Silence and non-verbal cues* : reducing reliance on teacher talk by encouraging teachers in the proper use of pauses and in the effective use of facial expressions, body movement, head movement, and gestures.

(e) *Reinforcing student participation* : encouraging students to respond through the use of praise and acceptance as well as non-verbal cues such as nodding and smiling.

(f) *Fluency in asking questions*: eliminating unnecessary hesitations and repetitions of questions.

(g) *Probing question* : skill in framing questions which lead students to elaborate on, or raise the level of, their responses.

(h) *Higher order questions* : questions which elicit responses that require higher intellectual levels from students instead of responses that involve only fact stating or descriptions.

(i) *Divergent questions*: Questions which elicit student responses that are unconventional, imaginative and cannot be judged simply to be correct or incorrect.

Other skills to become incorporated in the Stanford list were "recognizing attending behaviour", "illustrating and use of examples", "lecturing", "planned repetitions", and "completeness of communication" (Allen and Ryan, 1969).

As an indication of the widespread adoption of the concept of technical skills of teaching, institutions as far apart as the University of Stirling in Scotland and the University of Sydney in Australia implemented teacher education programmes incorporating them.

An Australian team of authors (Turney *et al.*, 1973) developed a system for classifying teaching skills under which seven categories emerged. These were :

(a) Motivational skills, including reinforcing student behaviour, varying the stimulus, set induction encouraging student involvement, accepting and supporting student feelings, displaying warmth and enthusiasm; and recognizing and meeting students' needs.

(b) Presentation and communication skills, including explaining, dramatizing, reading, using audio-visual aids, closure, using silence, encouraging student feedback, clarity, expressiveness, pacing, and planned repetition.

(c) Questioning skills, including refocusing and redirecting, probing, high-level questions, convergent and divergent questions, stimulating student initiative.

(d) Skills of small group and individual instruction, such as organizing small group work, developing independent learning counselling, encouraging co-operative activity and student to student interaction.

(e) Developing student thinking, such as fostering inquiry learning, guiding discovery, developing concepts, using simulation, role playing and gaming to stimulate thought, developing student problem solving skills, encouraging students to evaluate and make judgments, and developing critical thinking.

(f) Evaluative skills, including recognizing and assessing student progress, diagnosing learning difficulties, providing remedial techniques, encouraging self-evaluation, and handling evaluative discussion.

(g) Classroom management and discipline, including recognizing attending and non-attending behaviour, supervising class group work, encouraging task oriented behaviour, giving directions, and coping with multiple issues.

Turney *et al.* (1973) provided a useful list of references relevant to each broad category of skills but pointed out that there were some difficulties in documenting evidence of the validity of the specific skills nominated.

Similar selections of technical skills of teaching have been employed in micro-teaching and mini course programmes in many different countries. Many of these became incorporated in the movement known as "performance-based" or "competency-based" teacher education. Allen (1994) gave following families of Microteaching skills.

1. Questioning Skills

- *Number of Questions*

  The introductory questioning skill. Frequency and total number of questions without any judgment of quality. Attention is also given to the spread of questions to all members of the class.

- *Open-ended Questions*

  Questions which have no specific answer.

- *Higher Order Questions*

  The skill of asking questions which have no set or defined answer which encourage thinking and require students to speculate and offer opinions.

- *Probing Questions*

  Reaching deeper levels of student awareness, often encouraging students to become aware of new issues and/ or positions.

- *The Framing of Questions*

  How a question is asked is crucial to its contribution to the learning process. Clarity is a most important requirement.

2. Reinforcement and Control

- *Positive and Negative Reinforcement*

  Techniques of reinforcement, positive and negative, with an emphasis on the value of positive reinforcement.

- *Verbal and Non-verbal Reinforcement*

  Both verbal and non-verbal cues from both students and teachers are integral to the teaching learning process

- *Encouragement*

  The skill of encouraging all students, weak and strong. Encouragement stimulates higher levels of performance.

- *Cueing*

  The skill to get a positive answer from any student, regardless of how reticent or confused he/she may be.

- *Silence*

  Using silence as a tool for control and emphasis. Both positive and negative reinforcement can be given.

- *Selected Student Focus*

  The ability to individualise instruction by selecting one or more students on which to focus attention and provide extra help.

- *Eye Contact*

  Eye contact compliments a learner, encourages attention, and provides the teacher with valuable information for continuous assessment.

- *Observation*

  Becoming more alert to the physical and social environment of the classroom.

- *Conflict Resolution*

  Alternatives for responding to negative or unwanted situations in the classroom, and resolving conflicts between students, most often verbal disagreements which become unproductive.

3. Examples

- *Relevant Examples*

  Selecting and using effective examples. All new learning is built on previous knowledge and experience.

- *Analogies and Metaphors*

  The use of analogies and metaphors to enhance learning.

- *Instances and Non-instances*

  Building learning from the concrete to the abstract and from the abstract to the concrete. Both are important teaching strategies to learn and use.

- *Concrete-abstract Continuum*

  Learning can proceed either from the abstract to the concrete or the concrete to the abstract and both strategies are appropriate.

4. Teaching Aids

- *Artifacts*

  Artifacts are defined as casual objects already available in the environment and require minimal modification for use in the lesson. Effective artifact use makes learning more vivid and memorable.

- *Teaching Equipment*

  Equipment which is either developed specifically for classroom use or is provided through formal acquisition.

- *Overhead Projector*

  Effective overhead projector skills.

- *Chalkboard*

  Effective chalkboard skills, making chalkboard use both simple and varied.

5. Teaching Aids

- *Lesson Introduction*

  How to begin a lesson effectively to gain student interest while focusing attention on the objectives of the lesson.

- *Lesson Closure*

  Effective conclusions to focus concept retention.

- *Assessment*

  Continuous assessment must become a habit for all teachers, and is the form of assessment most integral to microteaching.

6. Co-operative Learning

- *Paired Learning*

  This is the form of co-operative learning most appropriate for the microteaching setting. Many principles of co-operative learning can be demonstrated in a paired learning context.

- *Group Learning*

  Groups of two or more can be assigned learning tasks independent of teacher presentation.

- *Group Monitoring*

  The role of the teacher is to facilitate group learning, and the monitoring process should encourage trial and error learning.

7. Learning Principles

- *Deduction*

  Deductive learning does not produce few knowledge, but organises existing knowledge in more useful way.

- *Induction*

  Based on existing knowledge new knowledge can be incrementally developed.

- *Intuition*

  The most important new knowledge is based on intuition and the formation of hypotheses to be tested.

- *Falsification*

  Once new knowledge is proposed, the most important method of testing its validity is to try to find counter examples or exceptions. This is an important component of thinking skills.

- *Planned Repetition*

  Repetition is an important source of earning. Knowledge is "set" through repetition and the exploration of alternative examples.

- *Vividness*

  When a concept stands out in a learner's mind, it is remembered easier and longer.

- *Juxtaposition*

  Placing ideas, events, or objects in unusual relationships to each other enhances vividness and long-term learning.

- *Delayed Response*

  Learning to wait for 2 or more seconds before responding as a means of encouraging student reflection.

- *Stimulus Variation*

  Use of a variety of gestures, movement around the classroom, incorporating visual stimuli, and other sensory variation enhances learning.

Dunkin (1976) argued that two criteria should be applied in judging the validity of technical skills of teaching. The first was the extent to which the specific aspect of teaching behaviour was distinct from other aspects of teaching. Observers should be able to agree on what constitutes the nature of the skill and should be able to identify it when it occurs. The second criterion was the extent to which the skills had been shown to enhance student learning.

In his review of lists of technical skills of teaching, Dunkin (1976) found cause for optimism that specific classroom behaviours commonly associated with teaching skills could be distinguished reliably by trained observers.

A series of correlational studies, showing substantial relationships between microteaching performance and subsequent classroom performance has appeared (Brown, 1975). These may be interpreted as suggesting that microteaching does affect classroom performance, or equally plausibly, as providing a simple indication that those participants who can demonstrate skilled performance in microteaching can also do so in a classroom setting.

The pre-experimental approach is represented in the work of Borg (1972). In this study a group of in-service teachers were videotaped in their classrooms to allow a pre course evaluation of skill usage. The group then undertook a microteaching course and were videotaped again one week after the course, four months later, and 39 months later. It was shown that classroom performance immediately after microteaching is marked by greater skill use than before microteaching, that there is no significant regression in skill use after four months, and that after 39 months, performance remained significantly superior to pre microteaching performance in 8 to 10 skill-related measures.

One of the negative outcome investigations was that by Copeland and Doyle (1973). They compared the effects of a six-week microteaching treatment (focusing on three questioning skills) with the effects of a control treatment not related to microteaching or to the three teaching skills. The reported outcome of this study was that microteaching did not have a significant effect on classroom performance. However, inspection of the reported data indicates that individual differences among the seven subjects in each group are very substantial, and a partial reanalysis of the data (MacLeoad 1981) reveals that significant differences in favour of the microteaching group may be produced by controlling for overall frequency of questioning.

Two further studies involving Copeland (1975, 1977) report that the main effect of microteaching on subsequent classroom performance are not significant. However, the second study does show to significant interaction effects involving microteaching training, and this suggests that microteaching training may lead to skill acquisition but not necessarily to subsequent skill performance.

An experimental study finding positive outcomes of microteaching was that by Raymond (1973). She compared the classroom skill performance of a group who had received microteaching skill practice with a group who had not. It was found that the microteaching group did differ significantly from the control group on two of the three skill criteria, and on four other measures of teacher behaviour.

One of the comparisons in a complex but elegant and carefully controlled experimental investigation by Levis *et al.* (1974) was between a group participating in a normal school experience programme and a group undertaking a microteaching programme in a school setting. All participants in the study were given identical skill training. At the end of the training programme, all participants taught a 10-minute lesson to a class of five pupils and measures of skill acquisition were derived from this. On two of the three criterion skills the microteaching group significantly out performed the school experience group.

Butts (1977) compared a group of students receiving microteaching practice of questioning and responding skills with a group of students who did not receive such practice. On a pre-test, there were no systematic differences between the groups: on a post-test, 15 of the 16 criteria favoured the microteaching group, and these differences were statistically significant for the questioning skill components.

2.2 Supervision of Practicum

The practicum in teacher education is conducted under a variety of names. Common among the terms used are practice teaching, in-school experience, teaching rounds, and student teaching. Whatever the name, the essential element of the operation is that student teachers attempt to apply in school settings certain of the ideas propounded in teacher education courses. If, as the research indicates, practice teaching is the single most powerful intervention in a teacher's professional preparation, then the supervision of the student teacher is the single most powerful process in such intervention. Besides underscoring the importance of the work of supervisors, the research literature also reveals how potentially complicated and difficult supervision is.

While various people in the school such as the principal and subject teacher, as well as the pupils, inevitably become involved in the students' practicum experience, the personnel most directly involved with supervision are typically the tertiary supervisor and the co-operating teacher.

Turney *et al.* (1982) reports that research has found the influence of the co-operating teacher to be strong on both the attitudes and the teaching of student teachers. He finds it, therefore, paradoxical that co-operating teachers are so often arbitrarily selected and unprepared for their role. Turney provides an extremely comprehensive review of research on both co-operating teachers' and tertiary supervisors' influence, concluding that both have "considerable immediate influence on the developing professional attitudes and teaching styles of student teachers".

Coulter (1975) found that co-operating teachers and tertiary supervisors often have vastly different frames of reference about what constitutes effective teaching.

A study by Tuckman and Oliver (1968) found that the failure of supervisors to use common frames of reference when communicating with students about their teaching performances actually caused supervisor feedback to have a negative effect upon subsequent teaching performance.

Nias (1976) undertook a study which omitted the tertiary supervisor from the supervision process and noted that co-operating teachers and student teachers developed a trusting relationship and a candid and constructive approach to the critical appraisal of performance. However, co-operating teachers still needed opportunities to discuss and examine the implications of their role with the tertiary institution.

A number of investigations have indicated that the attitudes of student teachers tend to move during teaching practice in the direction of those held by their co-operating teachers (Price, 1961; Finlayson and Cohen, 1967; Johnson 1968; Yee, 1969; Cohen 1969; Peters, 1971). They alert teacher education programmes to the need to select only those co-operating teachers who have positive attitudes towards children, enlightened educational ideas and a commitment to teaching. Great damage could well be done by consistently placing students with teachers who do not hold these views.

The co-operating teacher's supervisory style itself has been shown to have a strong relationship with the work and interpersonal environment encountered in supervision. An early study by Blumberg and Amidon (1965), using Flanders' concepts for categorising teacher behaviours, examined the relationship between two dimensions of supervisory style, directness and indirectness, and aspects of student teacher behaviour. They found that supervision exhibiting the greatest incidence of high direct and high indirect behaviours or low direct and high indirect behaviours produced more favourable student teacher reactions on the productivity, communications, and learning scales than did other supervisory styles. A second study by Blumberg revealed that supervisory styles that emphasised indirectness produced a more positive perception of the interpersonal relationship between the supervisor and student teacher. Subsequently Blumberg and Weber (1968) examined the relationship between supervisory style and student teacher morale. They concluded that level of morale declined with perceptions of supervisory styles in the following order : low direct, low indirect; and low direct, low indirect. That is, the supervisory style which emphasised indirectness was accompanied by higher scores on morale as perceived by student teachers.

In one study Poole (1972) concluded that the establishment of a good working relationship, marked by mutual respect between the co-operating teacher, student and class is of utmost importance in determining satisfaction with the practice teaching situation.

Many studies have tended to confirm that the actual teaching behaviour of student teachers seems to be influenced greatly by that of their co-operating teachers. For instance, Joyce and Harootunian (1967), Yee (1969), and Wragg (1970) found that the teaching of most student teachers closely reflected the methods used by their co-operating teachers rather than those suggested in the teacher education programme. Flint (1965) found patterns of relationships between even the verbal classroom behaviour of co-operating teachers and their student teachers during a short teaching practice, but these patterns did not seem to have a longterm influence.

It is not surprising that in her analysis of the power relationship between student, co-operating teacher, and tertiary supervisor, Barrows (1979) notes that there is a hierarchical relationship with the co-operating teacher in the position of most power and influence over the student teacher. Many student teachers also believe that co-operating teachers disapprove of ideas and methods advocated by the teacher education programme (Shipman, 1967; Cope, 1971a, 1971b; Therrick, 1971). Because of such factors student teachers may think it prudent to be seen to reject much of what they have learned in their teacher education programme.

As Nias (1977) points out, there is little conclusive evidence that really lasting attitudinal and behaviour changes are brought about by practice teaching. Indeed exposure to a variety of teaching models during practice teaching periods can be beneficial to the students' professional growth.

Given the weight of evidence underlining the potential influence of cooperating teachers, a number of studies have investigated the nature and effectiveness of their supervision, as perceived by both student teachers and cooperating teachers themselves. These studies are useful in that they often reveal an interesting mismatch of perceptions and expectations between student teachers and their supervisors. For example, Fitch (1970) explored the perceptions of the two groups about supervisory tasks and their implementation. Among the conclusions he reached were the following, (a) Both groups preferred the supervisor's help to be of a practical nature, but only the supervisors saw their actual performance to be theoretical. (b) Both groups preferred and believed that student teachers were working out their own solutions of their teaching problems. (c) Although it was more true for supervisors than students, both groups preferred a directive, prescriptive supervising teacher. (d) Both groups saw supervising teachers to be non-directive and open. (e) While both groups saw students receiving the least help with planning, they both agreed that it was a desirable task. (f) Supervising teachers did not see themselves providing student teachers with an analysis but wished that supervisors provided such feedback.

In another survey McCurdy (1962) examined relationship between the amount of help that was needed by student teachers and the amount of help was provided by supervising teacher. Her findings included : (a) Students required "much" help and were given "much" help in handling disciplinary problems and in recognising individual differences. (b) Students wanted considerably more help with developing self expression, voice, poise, and emotional control than they felt they had received. (c) While the supervising teachers felt that the students only needed "some" help with evaluating pupils and products and having parent/teacher/child conferences, the student teachers wished there had been more help. (d) Students felt they had not received sufficient help in understanding professional activities, school policies, and the school programme.

Another investigation undertaken by Nicklas (1960) sought to identify those supervisory techniques regarded as effective or ineffective by student teachers and co-operating teachers. The main results of this study were: both supervising teachers and student teachers approved of private conferences, group conferences, teaching demonstrations, special duties, methods classes and tape recordings of lessons.

A study by Loadman and Mahon (1973) explored the relationship between student teacher rankings of the supervisory effectiveness of co-operating teachers and their attitude toward education. Results indicated that student teachers tended to perceive those supervising teachers espousing either highly progressive or highly traditional attitudes as less effective supervisors. The very effective supervisors were seen to be teachers who did not strongly support progressive educational views.

Finally, Switzer (1976) surveyed student teacher perceptions of supervising teachers' level of helpfulness in 60 specific behaviours which could be grouped into six areas — supervisory techniques, professional attitudes, pedagogical skills, planning skills, knowledge of children and human relations skills. He found that student teachers felt they had received most help from their supervising teachers in the area of knowledge of children. They also rated highly the human relations skills of supervisors. The areas most in need of attention were seen to be planning skills and the general supervisory techniques of the teachers. The 10 planning skills in order of most need of attention were :

(a) establishing behavioural objectives;

(b) knowing that progress sensibly step by step;

(c) developing lessons appropriate to goals;

(d) constructing lesson plans;

(e) employing efficient methods for changing activities;

(f) providing for motivation;

(g) using of visual aids;

(h) establishing of long-range goals;

(i) capitalizing on outside experiences;
(j) selecting of materials or activities.

The 10 supervisory techniques which could well be improved upon were, in order of most need for attention :

(a) taping a lesson for later discussion;
(b) listing expectations at the beginning;
(c) discussing planned induction process;
(d) giving feedback on lesson plans;
(e) discussing avoidance of common difficulties;
(f) holding conferences;
(g) appropriate demonstration teaching;
(h) clarifying expectations for teachers and pupils;
(i) giving honest but balanced feedback;
(j) gradual but comfortable induction.

General suggestions for improving the work of co-operating teachers have been made by Trimmer (1961) and Johnson and Knaupp (1970). They urge that co-operating teachers should provide students with an opportunity to develop their own style, and that while teachers should permit students to plan and execute teaching strategies and learning experiences, they should be readily able to give technical advice to assist the students' work. In particular, there is a need to give student teachers adequate information on the abilities, attitudes, and skills of the pupils at the beginning of the practicum so that the students will have realistic expectations of initial pupil performance and potential.

There is, too, evidence to indicate a dissonance between the views on supervision held by tertiary supervisors and students. Stewig's study (1970) of student teacher expectations indicates that they felt it was most important that supervisors are aware of, and provide for, individual differences between students; have an objective perception of the classroom situation and the ability to communicate this perception to student teachers and a sincere and positive attitude. Primary supervisors considered that their most important task was to conduct three-way conferences with student, co-operating teacher, and supervisor, while for secondary supervisors the most important task was to stimulate students to evaluate their teaching behaviour. Stewig concluded that "critical differences existed between the perceptions of (tertiary) supervisors and students that may have hindered communication and limited supervisory effectiveness".

Contextual Supervision, derived from Hersey and Blanchard's (1977) original Situational Leadership model, and reflecting elements of Glickman's (1990) Developmental Supervision model and Glatthorn's (1990) Differentiated Supervision model, is a leadership approach that promotes the professional growth of participants. In the Contextual Supervison model, individuals in a supervisory role match their supervisory styles to the contextual variables characterizing supervisees' situations (Ralph, 1992, 1992-1993, 1993a, 1993b).

Contextual Supervision emphasises that supervisory decisions must be based upon universally accepted human values such as honesty, integrity, and a respect for the sacredness of the person. The two values of justice and beneficence form its foundation. Justice refers to the fair treatment of, and respect for, the integrity of the person, and beneficence is defined as the virtue stressing the welfare of the person being helped (Frankena, 1973; Sergiovanni, 1992). Acting upon this moral foundation and taking into consideration the situational context, supervisors determine the specific development level of supervises in the particular professional skill being learned or practiced at the time, and match their leadership style to that level.

Veal and Rikard (1998) surveyed co-operating teachers' perspectives on the student teaching as follows. Student teaching has been the capstone experience in teacher preparation for more than 75 years. Welborn (1920) noted that by 1920, one-third of the normal schools placed student teachers in public schools. With few exceptions, the situation today is similar. Griffin (1989) concluded that student teaching was business as usual and that the triad of university – based supervisor, school-based co-operating teacher, and student teacher has remained stable over many years. Hierarchical decision-making in student teaching is a particularly constant characteristic. Co-operating teachers are excluded from many decisions; university personnel typically influence decisions about the choice of co-operating teacher, the duration of student teaching, the requirements of planning and written work, and the final grading (Glickman & Bey, 1990). Smyth (1986) viewed hierarchical relationships in many aspects of public education as problematic: Arguably the most serious issues confronting teachers are not matters of teaching technique, but impediments that exist because of power relationships.

Researchers have studied relationships within the three-person triad (Karmos & Jacko, 1977; Yee, 1968) and focussed on the interpersonal dimension within the triad (Bain, 1991; Barrows, 1979; McIntyre & Morris, 1980) primarily from the perspectives of university supervisors and student teachers. Researchers have recently examined the student teaching experience from co-operating teachers' perspective (Koerner, 1992; Rothman, 1981; Tannehill, 1989).

Numerous studies of the relationship between student teachers and co-operating teachers (Kremer-Hayon & Wubbels, 1992; Lemma, 1993) exist. Researchers have focussed on student teachers perceptions of co-operating teachers (Kagan, 1987; Karmos & Jacko, 1977; Rikard & Knight, 1997), the influence of co-operating teachers on student teachers (Bunting, 1988; Yee, 1969), and changes in student teachers' perspectives, skills, or attitudes (Ellwein, Graue, & Comfort, 1990; Griffin, 1989).

Studies focusing on the relationship between university supervisors and cooperating teacher (Horton & Harvey, 1979; Tannehill & Zakrajsek, 1988) provide examples of how the former can train the latter. Hoy and Woolfolk (1989) concluded from their literature review that little evidence exists of co-operating teachers and university supervisors working together to provide a quality student teaching experience. On the contrary, Glickman and Bey (1990) and McIntyre (1984) substantiated conflict between co-operating teachers and university supervisors in their literature reviews. Koehler (1988) decried the lack of reciprocity in her relationship as university supervisor with co-operating teachers due to her inability to spend the time needed to build trust. Tensions have often existed between university supervisors and co-operating teachers for a number of well-documented reasons. Researchers have written little about successful triads.

Lack of agreement about the roles triad members should play (Bain, 1991; Grimmit & Ratzlaff, 1986; Kauffman, 1992; Rothman, 1981) and lack of clarity about the goals of student teaching (Gallemore, 1981; Griffin, 1989; Marrou, 1989; McIntyre, 1984) may be reasons for the tensions researchers cite. Communication problems among all three members are also cited as a major source of tension (Bain, 1991; Kauffman, 1992; Koehler, 1988; Ryan, 1982). In one survey of co-operating teachers, the most common problems between co-operating teachers and student teachers were personal and related to communicaiton (Sonthall & King, 1979).

Zimpher, deVoss, and Nott (1980) noted that the chief activity of the university supervisor was to define and communicate university purposes and expectations for the student teacher and co-operating teacher. Mayer and Goldsberry (1993) assert that the university supervisor's task is to diffuse interpersonal tensions between the co-operating teacher and student teacher, clearing the way for the student teacher's growth. Boydell (1986) reached a slightly different conclusion about communication issues after her review of the literature : University supervisors use distancing devises such as avoiding controversial debate in order to sustain the complex working relationships within the triad. Rothman (1981) investigated, through critical-incident technique, behaviours co-operating teachers believed most and least effective by university supervisors and found that co-operating teachers most value having conferences with the university supervisor. She identified unclear triad roles and unclear goals in student teaching as the two most intense areas of interpersonal conflict. She concluded that conflicts between the two often resulted in competition for control between the co-operating teacher and university supervisor. Her findings confirmed what Yee (1968) had found much earlier: Triad relationships more often resemble competitive triad settings that co-operative triad situations. Shipman (1967) and Derrick (1971) independently identified that student teachers believe co-operating teachers disapproved of ideas and methods advocated by university teacher education programmes. An examination of the dynamics within three-person groups provides a possible explanation for the tensions among triad members described in the literature. Several researchers have viewed the student teaching triad through the lens of sociological triad theory concerning conflict in three-person groups (Barrows, 1979; Rothman, 1981; Yee, 1968).

Several studies have sought to discover whether the involvement of tertiary supervisors really enhances student teachers' experience. An investigation by Stapleton (1965) indicated that intensive supervision by tertiary staff, contrasted with their normal involvement, did result in better performance by student teachers. However, Morris (1974) found there was no significant difference between the classroom performance of student teachers who were supervised by university staff and those who received supervision entirely from school staff, except that the self-ratings of the former group suggested they were performing better than were the other group. There was also no significant difference between the two groups in their adjustment to the school situation, except that the university-supervised group seemed to have better rapport with co-operating teachers.

Other studies have been concerned with the work of tertiary supervisors and the self-concept, creativity, and anxiety of student teacher. In one investigation Burgy (1973) sought to identify the situational components and supervisory practices that lead to the development of a strong, positive self-concept in student teachers, believed to be most important in teaching success. While she found that in general there was no significant change in student teachers self-concept during teaching practices, three factors were identified as being associated with an increase in self-concept during teaching practice : (a) socio-economic status of the student teacher's classroom (heterogeneous classes produced greatest increase in student teacher self-concept, low socio-economic status some increase, and higher status a decrease); (b) the tertiary supervisor's with more than six years teaching experience showed the greatest increase in self-concept; and (c) supervisory practice of college supervisors (student teachers whose supervisors always scheduled their observations well in advance showed a marked increase in self-concept).

There has been a considerable interest in developing creative teachers. According to Cicirelli (1969) this concern has implications for the supervision of student teachers. Through their "diagnostic feedback", supervisors can either restrict the range of teaching behaviour of students or encourage them to explore a full range of teaching behaviour. He argues for the use of creative supervisors who would be more flexible, more sensitive to problems, more theoretical in orientation, and less interested in details. In a subsequent study Cicirelli explored the relationship between the creative ability of tertiary supervisors and the kind of diagnostic feedback given to student teachers, as revealed in their written reports on observations of the students' performance. He found that the more creative supervisors were aware of a greater number of factors in a student teacher's performance. They tended to use broad general factors in assessing a student teacher's performance rather than specific, detailed ones, and were more sensitive to factors involving pupil-teacher relationships than were their less creative colleagues. One of the most striking findings was the tendency for less creative supervisors to give specific prescriptions for the improvement of the lesson, while the more creative supervisors tended to see the lesson more in terms of its general objectives, planning, and organisation.

Practice teaching is an anxiety-producing experience for student teachers, even though studies have recorded some decrease in anxiety during practice teaching periods (Poole and Gaudry, 1974; Nicoll, 1975). Within the practice teaching experience, supervision has been shown to be an important stress factor (Yee, 1968). Research by Sinclair and Nicoll (1981) suggests that the act of being supervised by tertiary personnel was the source of tension, not necessarily the relationship between student and supervisor. As the investigators pointed out, "Many of the students resented the supervisor's evaluative function while finding the supervisor as a person supportive and helpful. The supervised lesson was generally viewed as being different from other lessons and students went to extraordinary trouble to prepare and execute such lessons..." More generally, high anxiety levels and confusion were promoted where a conflict existed between the teaching ideals of the supervisor and co-operating teacher with student torn between conflicting advice and criticism from the two.

As mentioned research has drawn attention to the high levels of stress among student teachers during the practicum. Coulter (1974) supported this in term of lowered self-image when students are moved into more difficult and unfamiliar teaching situations. He made the point that a deliberate attempt should be made to place students in teaching situations which are appropriate to their stage of professional development.

An investigation by Lowther (1968) indicated that student teachers want from co-operating teachers not only clear and consistent expectations, positive feedback, and careful evaluation, but they also want a professional relationship to be established which includes a generous amount of trust, support, understanding and consideration. This point is further emphasised in the study by Love and Swain (1980) who conclude that student teachers desire a co-operating teacher who offers constructive criticism, who shares ideas and materials with them, and provides such opportunities and support that they can experiment, innovate, and develop teaching strategies on their own initiative.

Considered in the light of student concerns, supervision will fundamentally become an exercise in human relationships. Technical expertise in strategies of supervision would seem useless it is combined with sensitivity to individual students and their unique learning requirements (Lomax, 1973).

A final interesting aspect of student's views on supervision relates to the expectation some have of the school principal. Nias (1977) has reported that student teachers expect the principal to be able to offer them support by (a) clarifying and articulating the philosophies and objectives of the school; (b) holding professional discussions with student teachers; and (c) helping when classroom relations with the teacher breakdown.

Research has pointed to the need for closer co-operative relationships within the supervision setting. To help overcome these significant shortcomings there is a need for more organised approaches to supervision which focus on the rigorous analysis of classroom teaching in a co-operative manner. One such organised approach involving a collegial relationship is that referred to as clinical supervision.

Clinical supervision has been defined as that approach to practicum supervision which "draws its data from first-hand observation of actual teaching events, and involves face-to-face (and other associated) interaction between the supervisor and teacher in the analysis of teaching behaviours and activities for instructional improvement" (Goldhammer *et al.* 1980). The principal emphasis in clinical supervision is on helping the student teacher focus on improving particular aspects of teaching through a systematic approach to the supervision task.

Since the early 1970s much progress has been made in the development of models which explain how the processes of clinical supervision might be followed. The work of Cogan (1973), Goldhammer *et al.* (1980), and Boyan and Copeland (1978) identified five stages in clinical supervision. In a pre-observation conference, stage 1, the supervisor and the student teacher discuss teaching plans, delineate areas to be focussed on during observation and ways in which observations will be recorded. In stage 2, the classroom observation phase, the supervisor carries out observations in the classroom and records data ready to discuss teaching issues with the student. During stage 3, the analysis and strategy phase, the supervisor and the student, separately, reflect upon what has happened during teaching and decide what issues could profitably be raised in discussions, particularly the strengths upon which the student should build. Stage 4 is the post-observation conference during which data are fed back to the student and discussions are made about future teaching. Finally in stage 5, the post-conference analysis, both the supervisor and the student reflect upon their professional behaviour and, especially, the supervision process itself.

The five stages described above can be expanded—Cogan (1973) has eight—but what is important is that a relationship is established which encourages clear communication, understanding, and mutual trust between the supervisor and the student. Thus supervisors must understand the importance of processes they are following in clinical supervision and they must possess specific capabilities including "skills which ensure clear communication and establish open and healthy interpersonal relations, skills in systematic and objective observation and analysis of classroom behaviours, and skills in conducting supervisory conferences, providing focussed databased feedback in a non-threatening manner, and facilitating growth in student teachers' problem-solving abilities" with greater and more systematic participation in the student teacher's professional development (Copeland and Boyan, 1975). Although such a concept of clinical supervision has been slow in gaining acceptance in preservice and in-service supervision of teaching, in the 1980s there have been developed a number of promising training programmes to facilitate the development of supervisor understanding and skill in the process (*e.g.*, Boyan and Copeland, 1978). One of the most sophisticated and comprehensive programmes has been designed by Turney and his associates (1982). These programmes combine handbook and television materials to provide a realistic and flexible resource for supervisor training. They focus on the process of clinical supervision and the skills inherent in the six key roles that supervisors perform—manager, counsellor, instructor, observer, provider of feedback, and evaluator on Criteria for Evaluating Teaching; Lesson Analysis; Supervision of Teaching; and Concepts of Teacher Education.

2.3 Induction of Beginning Teachers

According to Zeichner (1979), the two major types of induction programmes are internships and beginning teacher programmes. He concluded that internships were themselves confined to three major types-fifth year internships for liberal arts graduates, Internships as part of a five or six year integrated preparation programme and a Teacher Corps internship. McDonald (1982) defined internship as including :

> ...... at least half-time teaching of no less than five or six months with full responsibility assigned to the interns for the groups of classes which they teach.

Beginning Teacher : One who has completed all preservice training requirements (including student teaching); has been granted a provisional certificate; is in the employ of a school district; has generally the same type and degree of responsibility assigned to more experienced teachers— and is either in his or her first year of service to the profession or to a particular school district.

Beginning Teacher Programme : A planned programme which is intended to provide some systematic and sustained assistance specifically to beginning teachers for at least one school year. The persons providing the support are specifically assigned that responsibility (Zeichner 1979).

Zeichner (1979) helpfully reviewed the induction literature from the previous 15 years and studied 11 programmes, in detail. Grant and Zeichner (1981) reported the findings from a limited investigation into school-based induction for a representative sample of beginning teachers not involved in experimental programmes and described the support they actually received. Informal support was thought by the teachers to have been of benefit. Conversations with other teachers and friends were the most valued. Interestingly the great majority of teachers were generally satisfied with the kinds and level of induction support they received during their first year. The suggestions they had for improvement reflected a concern for immediate and specific problems to do with school setting, the classroom, and their teaching needs. A few wanted more release and planning time or more time for observing other teachers. Thirty-five teachers wanted more opportunities to receive curriculum information of a specific kind and 34 of a more general kind on school routine. Twenty-one wanted more in-classroom assistance from experienced teachers and, while most (85 per cent) had been at least once observed by their principal as part of a formal evolution; 79 per cent received no in-classroom assistance during the year; they therefore appeared to want in-classroom assistance of a non-evaluative kind.

McDonald (1982) reported on a major study that significantly, very few "real" intern programmes appeared to exist and McDonald concluded that they were not a major feature of United States teacher education. Three intern programmes were studied in depth. In addition to course work, the Stanford internship included responsibility for teaching two classes a day for a school year plus at least one hour daily in school for preparation, observation, and so on. The University of Oregon programme concentrated upon the preparation of elementary-school teachers and consisted of four terms of graduate study combined with a year of full-time teaching leading to a Masters degree.. At Temple University, the programme required a minimum commitment of two years during which time the intern worked as a full, salaried teacher and was also enrolled in a course work programme. All three programmes were selective in their recruitment and regarded the interns as a rather elite group. The Oregon programme emphasised clinical supervision, the Stanford programme used microteaching and at Temple the emphasis was on a humanistic approach to professional decision-making. According to the interviewees-interns, first year teachers, school district staff, and programme faculty—these three programmes had been successful and popular over the years. Yet few such programmes were identified and McDonald concluded that this was because of widespread professional organizational, and financial misconceptions about internship. The crucial factor was the nature and quality of the supervision provided within the school setting but the strength of the internship, the sense of reality which springs from teaching in one school, also prevented the intern from acquiring more broadly based experience in a variety of schools.

Taylor and Dale (1971) reported on a national survey of the probationary year. A representative sample (10 per cent) of the 1966 to 1967 cohort of beginning teachers (n=3,588) and found that more teaching practice was called for but the most commonly voiced complaint concerned the amount of time devoted to the methods of teaching main and subsidiary subjects, which was generally considered to be inadequate.

Tisher (1978, 1980) reported a national study carried out in Australia. At least 60 per cent of the beginning teachers recommended the adoption of the following induction procedures: receiving written materials on conditions of employment; receiving written materials on school matters; accepting advice in classroom management or help in producing programmes of work; accepting evaluation of own teaching; participation in organized consultation with experienced school personnel; attending group meetings for beginning teachers at school; observing other teachers' methods of teaching; visiting other schools for observation/consultation; conferring informally with beginning teachers from other schools; looking at local educational resources. With respect to research on induction, two broad groups of questions are pertinent within each country : (a) what is the nature and extent of the induction knowledge base ? and (b) more particularly, how satisfactory was the research methodology which provided it ? Next, can policy makers and practitioners make use of that knowledge ?

Zeichner (1979) concluded that good induction programmes should include : (a) additional release time for the beginning teacher; (b) school-based support from a colleague acting as a mentor or professional tutor who also receives some additional release time plus initial and continuing training; (c) planned and systematic school-based activities including classroom observation and support; (d) planned and systematic externally based activities organized by L.E.A. and college personnel; and (e) the explicit and active support of schools principals and L.E.A. administrators.

The following broad aim for induction programmes, drawn from the United Kingdom, finds explicit and implicit support from experience elsewhere :

> "All our evidence suggests both that the overwhelming concern of most probationers is with the practicalities of their own teaching situation. It is, therefore, recommended that the broad aim of the programme should be to offer practical and

individualised help to probationers and that the main focus should be upon the problems and opportunities facing them in their own classrooms and schools" (Bolam 1973).

As a result of the national pilot schemes, the evaluators recommend that induction programmes should provide information, advice, and in-service experiences to achieve following aims related to enabling teachers to make independent, professional judgments:

(a) the promotion of growth and development, not simply survival skills, for all beginning teachers;

(b) subject teaching skills;

(c) general teaching and classroom skills;

(d) colleague relationships;

(e) school procedures;

(f) L.E.A. procedures; and

(g) the teacher's personal situation.

A key question for all those, especially mentors or tutors, trying to help beginning teachers is how to provide effective help which is relevant to the needs of the beginning teacher in the classroom.

2.4 Mentoring

Mentoring in the preparation and education of teachers is of interest and concern in many countries. In the USA, mentoring plays an important role in the education of teachers (Little, 1992). In other countries including England and Australia, the time that pre-service or student teachers spend in schools on Initial Teacher Education (ITE) courses has increased in recent years (Department for Education, 1992; Tisher, 1995) accompanied by necessary redistribution of responsibility and resources from Higher Education Institutions (HEIs) to school. Schools and mentors are increasingly equal partners with the university in the preparation of new teachers. Some have greeted the shift with unreserved enthusiasm: It offers the opportunity for a quantum increase in the power and effectiveness of Initial Teacher Training (ITT) (Tomlinson, 1995).

The mentoring literature illuminates the roots of both the enthusiasm and the alarm. The inadequacy of theory-practice models of teacher education (Goodlad, 1990) and the increased adoption of reflective practice approaches to teacher education (Schon, 1987) concentrate attention on the work of schools in ITE. For some, the moves toward school-based training are the overdue empowerment of teachers as equal partners in the education of student teachers (Wilkin, 1992). Recent research into how student teachers learn to teach has increasingly emphasised the need for student teachers to recognise previously constructed images and beliefs about teaching and examine the impact of these history-based personal beliefs on their professional development (Calderhead & Robson, 1991; Cole & Knowles, 1993; Holt-Reynolds, 1992; Johnson, 1993; Watzlawick, 1978). This emphasis casts doubt on the applicability of traditional academic HEI (Higher Education Institutions) environments as conducive settings for learning to teach (Elliott & Calderhead, 1993).

Roles and Responsibilities of Participants

Furlong, Hirst, Pocklington, and Miles (1988) propose an analytical framework of four levels of learning for student teachers. They agrue that mentors and HEI tutors, because of their different areas of experience and expertise, have distinct but complementary professional roles and responsibilities in the education of student teachers. The mentor has most to contribute at levels of direct practice and indirect practice, whereas the HEI tutor has a greater contribution to make at levels of practical principles and disciplinary theory.

Using a framework of differentiated roles for the different personnel involved, Bennett and Dunne (1996) examine the extent to which the evidence of the mentoring process itself in a particular ITE partnership reflected these differentiated roles. They studied four student teachers in different schools over a 10-week teaching practice. Their findings indicate that, in general, the differentiated role structures set out in the partnership mentoring model and used to inform the mentor training programme, were being enacted successfully. "Class teachers focus largely on craft knowledge.... co-tutors concentrate on areas such as teaching dimensions, curriculum knowledge and subject matter knowledge, whereas supervisors, in seeking principle-oriented outcomes, relate more to children's learning and theories and research on teaching processes".

Several writers have developed models of the stages that student teachers typically go through in their professional development (Berliner, 1987; Fuller, 1969; Kagan, 1992). Berliner (1987) postulates five levels of teacher development, ranging from novice, through beginner, competent, and proficient teacher, to expert. Competent teachers tend to rely on a set of maxims or rules in their decision-making drawn from personal experience and the prevailing culture of teaching. Experts, on the other hand, tend to be improvisational performers (Borko & Livingston, 1989); their actions will depend very much on the circumstances of each situation.

Maynard and Furlong (1993) suggest five distinct stages of development that students and beginner teachers typically move through in learning to teach : early idealism, survival, recognising difficulties, hitting the plateau, and moving on. In facilitating development through these states, they conceptualise three models of mentoring: the apprenticeship model, the competency model, and the reflective model. They state that each mentor model is partial and inadequate, perhaps only appropriate at a particular stage of a trainee's development (Maynard & Furlong, 1993) and suggest that mentor development goes through a series of stages that mirror and operate in response to student teacher stages of development.

Approaches that focus on stages in student teacher development tend to emphasise professional development other writers have focused on the interpersonal aspects involved in mentoring and learning to teach. Brooks (1996) studied 150 mentors working on a 1-year postgraduate secondary ITE programme, asking them to prioritize the skills and qualities they regarded as most important to their role as mentors. She found that they gave highest priority to interpersonal skills (about 40 per cent frequency rating), over the importance given to professional experience, personal qualities, and subject-specific expertise. Clearly, the mentors believe the interpersonal elements of the relationship they establish with their student teachers are crucial.

Other writers have focussed on the mentoring relationship between mentor and mentee and the various stages that the relationship goes through (Kram, 1983; Phillips 1977). Work at Amherst, Massachustts, has identified three developmental stages in the mentor-student teacher relationship (Martin, 1994). First, in the formal stage, the student teachers present themselves as prospective teachers to mentors competent to help prepare them. The second stage is the cordial stage, characterized by growing trust and respect between mentors and student teachers on personal and professional levels. The mentors act as instructors and critics, instilling confidence as mentees go through inevitable disillusionment and doubt. Finally, in the friendship stage, the student teachers acquire the confidence to see themselves as budding teachers, with characteristically various effects. Student teachers may see little need for mentors any longer; mentors may withdraw and leave the student teachers autonomous too soon, which they may resent, creating feelings of being used; or mentors may resent the student teachers' growing confidence.

Mentoring relationships are much more complex than these typologies suggest, involving not only the personality of mentor and mentee (Turner, 1993), but also interpersonal or psychosocial development, career and/or educational development, and socialisation (Field, 1994) between individuals of different experience, expertise, and orientations. Although the quality of the relationships between student teachers and mentors is of crucial importance in mediating the quality of teaching practices (Bennett & Carre, 1993), the probability of difficulties is high (Wildman, Magliero, Niles, 1992), given these complexities in the relationship.

Personal Perspectives, Values and Assumptions

Some writers propose models of mentoring arising from how mentors approach their mentoring tasks. Many writers have drawn up comprehensive lists of different mentoring roles. Descriptions of these roles include parent figure, support system, trouble shooter, scaffolder, guide, counsellor, and role model (Abell, Dillon, Hopkins, McInerney, & O'Brien, 1995)

McNally and Martin (1997) conducted in-depth interviews with a small sample of mathematics mentors working on a 1-year postgraduate secondary ITE course. Working from Daloz's (1986) framework of support and challenge in mentoring, they developed three typologies of mentors. Type 'A' mentors stress the nurturing and supportive role of mentoring and take a laissez-faire, low-challenge approach that can serve to confirm the *status quo*. Type 'B' mentors combine high support with high challenge to empower student teachers to engage in learning to teach as a critically reflective process. Type 'C' mentors have a strong sense of themselves as authorities in the mentoring role but tend toward a lack of real engagement with the student teachers' needs, which may result in student teachers feeling unsupported and overwhelmed.

Saunders, Pettinger, and Tomlinson (1995), analyzing interviews with 32 prospective teacher mentors, have drawn up a loose typology of four orientations. The first type is the hands-off facilitator mentor who emphasises discussion with mentees rather than shared or team teaching. The notion of the mentees as autonomous, would be teachers developing their own potential underpins this orientation. The second type is the progressively collaborative mentor who emphasises working alongside mentees, offering advice as the confidence and skills of the mentees increase. The third type is the professional friend mentor who regards the student teacher as part of the school, emphasising the importance of the mentees' actual performance in the classroom, and often stressing this above the value of challenging or praising the mentee. The fourth type is the classical mentor who emphasises counselling techniques, listening to problems, and giving feedback.

That mentors hold predefined ideas about their role as mentors and that these orientations, far from being specific to mentoring, operate on a more general level should come as no surprise given much of the recent research identifying similar influences in learning to teach (Elliott & Calderhead, 1993). Facilitating teachers' professional development requires mentors to understand and engage in this process, helping their mentees unravel their preconceptions and examine the impact of these preconceptions on their developing practice, helping them refine or amend their perspectives as appropriate for teachers starting out on the mentoring role such a reflective stance is likely to be more realistic, more effective and more satisfying. It will help them to realise, for instance, that they have much knowledge and skill which is of relevance to mentoring (Tomlinson, 1995).

Haggerty (1995) focuses on conversations between mentors and student teachers in which they discussed the development of mentees' thinking on predetermined issues. Haggerty found that mentors were able to talk about their own practice, but they were less successful in talking about the practicability concerns they used in their decision-making. Instead of recognising and articulating the complexity of decisions teachers make, the mentors in this study tended to behave. As though it was unproblematic and uncontentious to implement recommended good practice (Haggerty, 1995). Similarly, Elliott and Calderhead (1993) conclude that mentors hold simplistic views about learning to teach, and Feiman-Nemser, Parker, and Zeichner (1993) show how mentors do not share their own thinking about lessons or rationales behind approaches they use. It would appear, then, not only that mentor orientations toward mentoring influence their practice as mentors, but the mentors themselves may not readily recognize, or make explicit, this process.

Dynamics in Mentoring Relationships

Daloz (1986) describes the characteristics of support and challenge and discusses ways in which these two can combine to enhance learning within mentoring relationships. He describes support as an affirming activity in which the learner feels cared for, whereas the functions of challenge is to open a gap between student and environment, a gap that creates tension in the student, calling for closure. In this definition of challenge, generating cognitive dissonance is the mainspring for learning; without such dissonance and the concomitant mitigation of pre-existing, images, knowledge acquired during preservice teacher education appears to be superficial and ephemeral (Kagan, 1992).

Feimen-Nemser *et al.* (1993), found that mentors fail to engage in critical discussion with their mentees. Haggerty (1995) studied conversations between mentors and student teachers and found that although mentors were successful in getting mentees to discuss their developing ideas, the mentors did not feel able to disagree with or challenge such ideas. Similarly, the student teachers believed that the only judgments they could make were ones with which their mentors were likely to agree. Booth (1993) found that mentors seemed to lack the confidence or expertise to tackle some critical issues with their student teachers or were simply unaware of the need to address such issues.

Cameron-Jones and O'Hara (1997) found, considerable agreement between students and classroom teachers about the supportive function of the teachers. Both parties found support as the primary feature of the relationship between teachers and students. There was less agreement about the place of challenge; both parties saw it as secondary to support, and students seemed unaware even of the amount of challenge that teachers felt they offered.

Ronnestad and Skovholt (1993) have carried out research into the supervision of beginning and advanced students in counselling. They conclude that for beginning students, supervision has an instructional, didactic, and skill focus; supervisors, although they should assist in maintaining an open and exploratory stance even when the focus may be on mastering techniques and methods, need to be aware of the natural tendency of students to simplify a complex professional world. Much of this resonates with the needs and perspectives of student teachers early in their professional development. As student gain experience, their relationship changes to become one more consultive (Kadushin, 1974) and egalitarian (Fisher, 1989). Ronnestad and Skovholt (1993) have observed a gradual awakening to the concerns of transference and counter-transference phenomena and a greater willingness (as they get more experience) among students to explore personal assets and limitations. However, in looking at the role of the supervisor at this stage of a student counsellor's development, Ronnestad and Skovholt point to issues potentially very relevant to teaching : A counsellor may assist the client towards increased self-awareness, which may be an aim in itself. The supervisor may assist the graduate student toward increased self-awareness as this relates to professional functioning. Clearly, if ITE aims to develop autonomous reflective teachers, mentors must engage with the individual student teacher and recognise his or her individual strengths and difficulties, not always readily expressed verbally, but perhaps manifest through the dynamics and operation of their relationship. Ronnestad and Skovholt (1993) conclude, 'at the advanced student level, in particular, the supervisor needs to take responsibility to create, maintain, and monitor the relationship with her or his student. The relationship can provide a structuring and process mediating role through the turmoil experienced by the student in practicum'.

Greater consideration of this relationship in mentoring research might help improve understanding of the mentoring process and offer the prospect of more effective mentoring in practice. Wildman *et al.* (1992) present the case for such an emphasis on mentoring relationships in strong terms by when they write, because mentoring involves highly personal interactions, conducted under different circumstances in different schools, the roles of mentoring cannot be rigidly specified. Therefore, it is a mistake to develop any external definition or conception of mentoring and impose it by means of political pressure or high powered staff development activity.

2.5 Indian Studies

The review of literature shows that some scattered efforts in this area have been made in India from time to time to improve teacher training but no comprehensive effort has been made to restructure teacher training. Practically at most of the teacher-training institutions in India Practice Teaching is on the traditional system. Regional Colleges/Institutes of Education (NCERT) have introduced Internship in Teaching but in modified form. Some studies conducted in India on teacher training and its components are as follows.

Jangira and Dhoudiyal (1981) designed class-questioning and behaviour observation system in which they indicated six dimensions, *i.e.* question, function, structural characteristics, delivery, distribution, pupils' response and its management. The study contributed very significantly to the considerations in modifying the classroom questioning behaviour of teachers.

Jangira, Singh and Matto (1980) studied the effectiveness of microteaching as means of improving teaching competence of in-service teachers. Paintal (1979-80) and Kaur (1980) developed self-instructional courses for improving the skills of questioning of teachers. Kaur prepared self-instructional audio cassettes for developing teaching skills. Mukhopadhyay (1981) compared the mutual effectiveness of Micro-teaching and Modular Approach and found both to be equally effective. Patel (1978), Ray (1978) Paikaray (1981) carried out research on different components of Micro-teaching.

Singh (1982) observed that the teacher educator and student-teacher ratio at an average was 1:12. Regarding qualification of teacher-educators, 6 per cent had Ph.D., 78.4 per cent M.A./M.Sc., 15.0 per cent were B.Ed. Chanday (1976) and Srivastava (1980) observed that academic achievement and teaching efficiency had positive relationship. Firm determination, dutifulness, disciplinarism, interest in teaching-job, and foresightedness were the five areas which determined the sense of responsibility. Teacher effectiveness and attitude towards teaching had been positively and significantly related with one another.

Das, Passi, and Singh (1976) studied the effectiveness of Micro-teaching as a technique of training teachers and tried out different variations of Micro-teaching Components to determine their relative effectiveness. The study emphasised that the student teachers trained through "Standard Micro-training" or Modified Standard Micro-teaching Techniques acquired higher general teaching competence as compared to the student teachers trained under the traditional teacher-training technique or the usual Practice Teaching Programme.

Mehrotra (1974) presented a paper on "Problem of Teacher Education in India". He attempted to introduce Programmed Learning and Educational Technology in teacher education. In this connection he felt these devices might be very helpful in student teaching programme. For this purpose he quoted various situations in student teaching where this device might be very fruitful.

Tiwari (1967) initiated a project on Micro-teaching in Government Pedagogical Institute at Allahabad. He found that Micro-teaching could be used profitably in the Training Institutions and in Secondary Schools. This would develop the student teacher's insight and would make them better qualified and better teachers. Shah (1970) tried an experiment with seven students of the ninth class. He used a tape recorder for recording the performance of a teacher. His conclusions were that the recording on the tape recorder and the listening to it afterwards helped the teacher in correcting his mistakes.

Chudasama (1971) tried out Micro-Teaching with students at the Faculty of Education and Psychology at CASE Baroda and found that Micro-teaching was more affective than the traditional technique in the development of indirect teacher behaviour. Pareek and Rao (1971) in their study designed the experimental group of 10 teachers who were exposed to ten days teaching programme on Interaction Analysis which emphasised feedback of classroom interaction behaviour through Flanders Interaction Category, their interpretations, experimentation with new behaviour patterns through Role Plays and actual Practice Teaching as inputs of treatment. It was found that due to training the experimental group started using more and more of "praising", "encouraging", "accepting" ideas and questioning compared to the control group of teachers as well as their own behaviour before training.

Jangira (1972) reported an experiment in modifying classroom behaviour of the teachers using feedback on F.I.A.C.S. He found that higher responsiveness, flexibility in teacher influence and indirectness resulted in higher adjustment, classroom trust behaviour and independence. Pangotra (1972) in an experiment to study the effect of different sources of feedback on student teachers found that feedback from supervisors was more effective than feedback from peers, researchers as well as pupils. Sharma (1972) in her experiment studied the effect of four different patterns of classroom behaviour of teachers on pupil achievement in relation to knowledge, comprehension and application as instructional objectives. Flanders, IACS. was used for training the teachers in the behaviour patterns selected for the treatment.

Marker (1972) conducted a comparative study of Micro-teaching and Conventional Practice Teaching of Pupil Teachers of Geography method. Their work was taped on a cassette tape recorder pin pointed on the five skills *viz.* (i) Set Induction, (ii) Stimulus Variation, (iii) Questioning, (iv) Response to Pupils' Answer, and (v) Closure. Significant improvement was obtained by the experimental group (Micro-teaching Group) as compared to the control group (Traditional Teaching Group). Reteach provided opportunity over learning which was important in gaining new skills. Dosajh (1973) conducted a study on change of teaching self concept through Micro-teaching with CCTV against the change in self concept through traditional method of Block Practice Teaching. Micro-teaching Group was found more efficient in teaching than the Traditional Group.

Marker (1973) submitted a report on an experiment in developing skills of classroom teaching of student teachers by simulation and new technique of supervision using checklist as an instrument. The science and mathematics group showed greater ability in the use of checklist than method masters of languages though there were some exceptions too and results were found encouraging.

Bawa (1984), studied the effect of Micro-Teaching with Planned Integration Training and found that exposure to Micro-Teaching resulted in improvement of teaching competence. Exposure to the integration based programme after Micro-Teaching did not result in wholesome and uniform improvement in teaching competence. Speed and presentation, and maintenance of discipline were the two component skills of general teaching competence which were not much affected by participation in integration-based instruction.

Bhatnagar (1980) in a review on studies and literature of Student Teaching and other practical work in the B.Ed. Programme in India concluded that the studies from 1952 to 1978 in this area had not concentrated on the practical work of the B.Ed. Programme. These studies emphasised the need for a comprehensive network of school activities to be included in student-teaching programmes. They highlighted the negligence in organisation of teacher-training institutions and their rigid structures. Micro-teaching as a popular concept of Teacher Training Programmes, gained ground in the seventies. NCERT produced workshop and seminar reports in the area of teacher-education during late seventies. A handful of studies were conducted on supervision of student-teaching programmes conducted by school principals and teacher-educators. No significant difference was observed in the case of supervision done by the principals and supervision carried out by teacher educators.

Bhatt (1966) developed and tried out a scheme for the qualitative improvement of teaching through training at Government Basic Training School, Kapasan. Besides getting training in planning lessons and teaching the teachers he also organised creative activities and training in Arts and Crafts. The Study revealed that as a result of training there was improvement in lesson planning and standard of teaching. On the basis of pre- and post-tests trainees' knowledge of the content was found to be much improved.

Bhattacharjee (1981) observed the effect of integrating a few selected teaching skills upon the teaching competence of B.Ed. Trainees. The study revealed that training for the integration of the four selected skills (introducing a lesson, fluency in questioning, increasing pupil participation, and using the blackboard) under the summative model of integration had contributed to the teaching competence of the experimental group significantly in comparison with the control group.

Chathley (1984) conducted an experimental study of teaching competency at Macro-level as a function of training in micro-skills among the prospective secondary school teachers in relation to skills and subject area. The finding indicated that there was significant improvement in the general teaching competence of trainees as a result of training in micro-skills and training in integrated skills. Among the trainees in physical sciences, the tetraclustered and hexaclustered strategies were more effective while among the trainees in languages the three strategies were equally effective in improving their general teaching competence. Among the social sciences trainees, the tetraclustered strategy was more effective than the biclustered and hexaclustered strategies in improving general teaching competence. For skill of explaining, introducing a lesson, reinforcement and blackboard use, the trainees in physical sciences gained quantitatively more than the trainees in social sciences and languages. For skill of fluency in questioning and achieving closure, the overall quantitative performance of male trainees was significantly better than that of their female counterparts, while for skill of blackboard use, the quantitative gain was more for female trainees. As a whole the trainees in physical sciences gained significantly more than trainees in social sciences and languages.

Deo (1985) studied the practical programme other than practice teaching in teacher education institutions and concluded that most of the student-teachers felt that "lack of time" was a major factor in not being able to achieve the objectives of practical programmes though they felt that a large number of practical programmes be incorporated in the training programme. For work experience and SUPW sufficient time and guidance were not provided to students by the teachers and there was no provision for them in the time-table. The student-teachers were not provided facilities for training in preparation of visual and audio aids. Physical education and participation in games and sports were taken casually by student-teachers. Excursions for student teachers were not arranged by the institutions. Social work had not been an integral part of the teacher-education programme. Co-curricular activities were not arranged according to the interests and needs of the students. Opportunities for talented students were not provided in the area of art, library, dramatic and other cultural areas. There was no provision for psychology practicals which could give student-teachers opportunity for application of theories of learning.

Dogra (1986) studied Effect of Training in Concept Development Strategies upon classroom communication behaviour patterns and found that student-teachers trained in the use of Content Analysis System showed a significant increase in defining, concrete examples, negative examples, amplification and vivid categories.

Simultaneously they showed a decrease in the use of background, naming, general examples, abstract examples, personal examples, digression and miscellaneous categories. The student-teachers trained in CAS presented the content by using different types of examples by enlarging the focus of attention, by relating or contrasting two or more things. As a result of training in CAS student-teachers showed an increase in the use of most of the relationship which were more emphasised during training. Teachers trained in the analysis of content communication could better engage themselves in self-evaluation.

Ekbote (1987) worked on development of a strategy for integration of skills in Teacher Training and found the integration strategy effective in student-teacher's performance in teaching. All the seven variables pertaining to the student-teachers, *viz.*, qualification, teaching experience, availability of study time, academic achievement, skill comprehension, attitude towards teaching and towards micro-teaching influenced the improvement in classroom teaching performance through the strategy. The experimental treatment included integration practice using instructional material, instructional techniques like discussion, lecture, simulated practice, classroom practice and field work as its components. The content units of the strategy were use of questioning and explaining, use of blackboard, use of visual media, reinforcement personalization, inquiry approach, variables influencing classroom teaching, diagnostic and remedial practices and organisation of co-curriculur activities related to classroom teaching.

Gupta (1983) studied the correlates of Teacher Performance in Simulated Teaching at Secondary Level. The main findings were that training in simulation technique resulted in significant gain in taxonomical performance and classroom performance rating of secondary science and mathematics student-teachers. When student-teachers were exposed to simulated teaching they gained in Indirect Teacher Talk, and lost in their Pupil-Initiative Ratio (PIR). Student-teachers with a high positive attitude towards teaching gave better performance through simulated teaching. Student-teachers of high academic ability showed the desired effect on their teaching behaviour or teaching performance through simulated teaching.

Kadwadkar (1984) had a critical enquiry into professional courses for college teachers in India and concluded that theoretical information, relating to "planning for teaching" ability and some components of teaching and testing abilities, was given in a global way and related practical work was either not prescribed or not given due weightage. No specific information relating to the ability, "dealing with behavioural problems of students in the classroom" was given. Some theoretical information relating to "Action Research" ability was given but no related practical work was attempted. Very little scope was given to demonstrate professional abilities. The main implications were suggested that the courses should be modified so as to make them performance-based; the micro-teaching approach should be used to upgrade the teaching competence of teacher candidates and more weightage should be given to practical work.

Kakkad (1983) studied Secondary Teacher Education Curriculum for developing Teacher Education Programme and came out with the findings that the duration of the Secondary Teacher Education Programme (STEP) should be two academic sessions. It should include educational theory, practice teaching, community work, work experience, sessional work and co-curriuclar activities. There should be content courses along with the school methodology paper. There should be two subjects for methodology of teaching and the number of lessons should be 15 for each subject. Internship in teaching should be introduced for a period of three months and there should be provision for urban and rural teaching in STEP.

Kalyanpurkar (1986) in a study on the effect of Micro- teaching in in-service teacher training programme found that Micro-teaching treatment had a positive significant effect on the development of skills *viz.* Probing Questions, Reinforcement, Explaining with Examples and Stimulus Variation. It has positive significant impact on pupils' attainment as well as on pupils' retention, pupils' liking for their teachers, and on the general competence of teachers. The implications were that Micro-teaching should find a place in in-service-teacher education programmes. General orientation in Micro-teaching techniques discussion of the skill to be practised relevant materials, demonstration of skills in simulated condition, discussion and observation, practice of the skills in simulated condition followed by regular teaching and opportunity to utilise the acquired skills in classroom situations should be included in teacher-training programmes.

Kudesia (1986) in a study of the teaching aspects as viewed by the Polytechnic Teachers of Induction Programme observed that the observes found their colleagues equally competent in two aspects of teaching, *viz.* introduction of lessons and use of methods and media, and least competent in summarizing the lessons. No significant differences were observed in the self-perception of trainees and observation of observers with respect to the competence of trainees in different aspects of teaching, in the perception of teacher-trainees belonging to different disciplines. The main aspects considered to be effective ways of teaching were that the objectives of the lesson should be stated clearly, the introduction of the lesson should be effective and interesting, the planning of the lesson should be on proper lines, the organisation and presentation of the subject-matter should be systemic and logical, examples and illustrations used during teaching should be relevant to the content, the selected teaching method should be suitable to the mental status of students, the teachers should use the media at relevant places, chalkboard work should be developed systematically and properly, the teachers' expressions and gestures should be appealing, the teacher should motivate students, presentation of information should be satisfactory, summarization of the main points of the lesson should be given to students on the basis of individual differences.

Mohanty (1984) studied Student Teaching Programmes in College of Education with special reference to Innovations in 19 Teachers Training Colleges in Orissa and found that training in technique of observation, maintenance of classroom discipline and organisation of functions and festivals were found in all the colleges. The criticism lesson and methods of teaching were poor. The Practice-Teaching Programme stressed delivery of lessons and no other activities expected from a student-teacher. Supervisors did not observe lessons completely. They rarely discussed their observation in lesson-plan journals with trainees. The evaluation was of doubtful validity as no evaluation criteria were explicitly stated. School-college co-operation was found poor in almost all institutions under study. The colleges lacked qualified method masters. The lecture method of teaching was in vogue. Micro-teaching and Team Supervision of Criticism Lessons were the only two innovations practiced in three colleges. In all respects, the functioning of government institutions was better than that of private institutions.

Naik (1984) in a comparative study of the effect of Micro-teaching and conventional approaches on Teaching competence observed that Micro-teaching Group scored significantly higher on pupils' perception, pupils' achievement and general teaching competence. It was difficult for a student-teacher to isolate skills as other skills interfered while practicing of them. Hence, it was suggested that instead of single skill practice, clusters of skills should be practised; and a unit to be taught during a 40 minute period should be given to a student-teacher throughout Micro-teaching lessons.

Natrajan (1984) in a study on competency-based programme in teacher education curriculum concluded that competency-based instruction proved suitable for teaching selected units in Instructional Planning and Administration. The seminar method seemed to be an effective method as it compared favourably with the competency-based approach. The lecture method was effective as a group method. Directed self-study did not compare well with other methods. There was a significant relation between self-esteem and acquisition of competencies. Attitude towards teaching methods had a favourable correlation with acquisition of competencies. The study proved that teacher education programmes could be made more effective through a competency-based approach.

Oak (1986) in a critical study of Micro-teaching techniques observed that while training the science student-teachers, activities such as teacher-talk, questioning, B.B. work and demonstration should be taken into account in preferential order. Mathematics teachers needed training, in order of priority, in activity such as explanation, questioning, and B.B. work. In the case of teaching of mother tongue, the order of priority was teacher talk, reading, recitation and questioning.

Passi, Singh and Sansanwal (1986) in a study on training strategies concluded that a student-teacher should reasonably distribute his practice teaching by judiciously selecting models of teaching from the four families. The present emphasis on Herbartian model should soon be replaced by evenly distributed efforts over the selected models. This would require an improvement and wide distribution of lesson plan guides, lesson plan formats and work-sheet, and other guide materials. Examiners of practice teaching should appreciate these new strategies of teaching. For the implementation of models of teaching the staffing pattern in teacher-education should be changed significantly.

Shah (1986) conducted a survey of management of student teaching in India which included 46 Secondary Teacher Training Colleges of 13 States of the country. The study revealed that a majority of the institutions favoured the objectives of development of competence in trainees to teach on the basis of accepted principles of learning and teaching. Demonstration lessons were used for orientation of trainees in the most of the cases. The overall picture was not impressive in regard to criticism lesson. Most of the institutions did not pay much attention to the content of the lessons. The lessons were evaluated through observation, value judgment and evaluation proforma. Unit planning and evaluation were used for preparation of lesson plans in most of the cases. In around 46 per cent of the institutions, model lesson plans were used for preparation of lesson plans. A large number of institutions favoured block practice teaching. Most of them had suggested the use of both internal and external evaluation. There was no common pattern followed on weightage given to different aspects of practice-teaching. Regarding the final evaluation, a team of supervisors evaluated the trainees performance in almost all institutions. Around one-third of them used the seminar method of teaching. Only 8 per cent provided training in the preparation of film strips. Rare use of CCTV and VCR was the common feature in teaching learning situations.

Sharma (1986), studied the effect of different Micro-teaching strategies on the development of probing question skill and verbal classroom interaction. It was concluded that the use of the standard method of Micro-teaching teach period for developing probing question skill was preferred. Exercise with reinforcement of the probing question skill behaviour was conducive to the growth of a teaching skill. Praising, encouraging, accepting or using pupils' ideas, questioning and learning were found to be significantly influenced by Micro-teaching treatments. Incidence of lecturing, the only one among the three direct behaviours decreased in consequence of the application of Micro-teaching treatments. Pupils talk response was influenced positively by Micro-teaching treatment.

Sidhu (1983), in a follow up study of different teacher training approaches found that Micro-teaching was superior to the conventional training approach in developing general teaching competency and professional teachers were found superior to novice teachers in GTC. There was no significant effect of training on the self-perception of the teachers about their own teaching effectiveness, and on the perception of the heads of schools with regards to their teaching effectiveness. It was suggested that instructional materials for different skills in the form of booklets should be prepared. Principals and teacher educators should be oriented in the new techniques of classroom interaction analysis, simulation, role playing and feedback.

In a study on the effect of training in teaching skills using micro-class, peers and real pupils on the general teaching competency. Singh (1984) observed that student-teacher trained using Micro-teaching under the simulated conditions acquired better teaching competency than those trained under the traditional training method. They acquired better teaching competencies who were trained for Micro-teaching in real classroom than those who were trained in simulated conditions, and Micro-teaching training developed in them positive attitude towards Micro-teaching.

Swami (1984), worked on diagnosis and remediation of deficiencies in basic understanding of prospective teachers and suggested that there is an imperative need to provide adequate bridge courses or parallel or inbuilt remedial courses in content as part of methodology course in B.Ed. programme to remedy deficiencies in the content to ensure reasonable mastery of the basics;

construction of diagnostic tests, preparation of detailed unit plans, self-instructional materials and to strengthen content-cum-methodology courses.

In a study of teaching competence of pre-service and in-service teachers trained through different treatments of Micro-teaching Syag (1984), observed that the Micro-teaching approach should be made on integral part of the student teaching programme. At least two continuous periods should be allotted for practicing skills in a Micro-teaching setting.

Teacher Training Institutions may use either peer feedback or/ and peer-cum-audio tape feedback during Micro-teaching treatment; and instructional materials on various teaching skills should be developed.

On the role expectations and the role performance of college supervisors on student teaching Teprongtong (1984) in a study found that the expectations of school principals, co-operating teachers and student-teachers did not differ on academic, skill development, guidance and overall supervisory role. Mean differences showed that student-teachers expected a liberal rather than a critical evaluation of student-teaching. The school principals and co-operating teachers were more concerned with the practical aspect of student teaching than the academic one and their expectations on the role of college supervisors of evaluation, of teaching skills, guidance and skill development were significantly higher than the academic role. Student teachers were more concerned with developmental help than academic help and critical evaluation.

In a trend report on research in teaching Passi and Sansanwal (1991) observed that for language teachers, the patterns of higher proportion of student talk to teacher talk, the flexibility, content cross and total teacher-talk were found to be normative expectations. Koul (1972) found that popular teachers distinguished themselves as more outgoing, intelligent, emotionally more stable, sober, conscientious, venturesome, tough-minded, strewed, placid, controlled and relaxed. Kulandaivel and Rao (1968) and Thakur (1976) identified qualities of a good teacher as rated by students as good teaching, kind and pleasing manners good advice and guidance to pupils, regular and punctual attendance and equal treatment to all. Maheshwari (1976), reported that effective teachers used the categories of "accepts feeling, praise, uses student ideas, questions, student response and initiation" whereas ineffective teachers employed "lecture, direction and authority" categories in their classroom behaviour.

General teaching competency, competency of teacher's concern for students, competency of using audio-visual aids, competency of professional perception, competency of giving assignments, competency of illustrating with examples, competency of pacing while introducing, logical exposition, classroom management, use of questions, initiating pupil participation, use of blackboard, recognising attending behaviour, competency of achieving closure were the desirable teaching competencies of an effective science teacher (Mathew, 1980). Passi and Sharma (1982) identified the teaching competencies of language teachers as giving assignment, loud reading, asking questions, introducing a lesson, managing a classroom, clarification, secondary loud reading, using the blackboard, using reinforcement, pacing, avoiding repetition, consolidating the lesson, dealing with pupils' responses, improving pupils' behaviour, audibility, using secondary reinforcement, recognising pupils' attending behaviour, presenting in verbal mode and shifting the secondary channel. Shukla (1981) identified teaching skills which were involved in the teaching of mathematics at the secondary school levels as skill of developing a concept, skill of developing a principle, skill of applying the inductive approach and deductive approach, skill of figure drawing and skill of applying problem solving approach.

Bhagoliwal (1982) found that more effective teachers were characterised by a fairly higher level of differentiation and integration in their cognitive and perceptual functioning. They had a superior capacity for imaginative and original thinking. More effective teachers had a well-developed value system and ego organisation. Intelligence, creativity and interests were characteristically interrelated in promotion of proficiency in teaching (Jain, 1977).

Gupta (1979) reported that blackboard work, correcting oral mistakes, explaining difficult points, general knowledge, handwriting, knowledge of the subject, maintaining discipline, power of oral expression, revision of main points, skill of questioning and use of material aids were found to be helpful in Teaching. Sharma (1977) reported that discussion was the most effective technique of providing feedback by the peer supervisors. Similarly written feedback was effective in the case of the skill of shifting sensory channels. Feedback by college supervisors brought better results than feedback by peer supervisors (Kanwal, 1979).

Vasistha (1976) reported that training in the Flanders Verbal Interaction Category system contributed significantly to the attitude towards teaching, self-perception and classroom performance of secondary science and mathematics student-teachers. The teaching behaviour of teachers could be changed in a positive direction if they were appraised with the sum total of their teaching in the form of feedback information by way of self-rating and class-rating (Mishra, 1985). The classroom behaviour of student-teachers in desirable directions could be modified through simulated social-skill training (Singh, 1979).

Singh (1974) observed that student teachers trained through Micro-teaching changed their verbal behaviour in the classroom. Vaze (1976) while studying the effects of modelling and micro-teaching on the acquisition of certain skill in questioning among student-teachers found that Micro-teaching was the best treatment for acquiring skill in asking probing questions. The symbolic modelling treatment did not differ significantly from audio-modelling treatment. Training in classroom questioning behaviour resulted in improved question delivery behaviour of teacher as well as improvement in pupil achievement (Yadav, 1983). The four-year integrated B.Ed. course was found to be effective in comparison to the traditional one year B.Ed. course in terms of teaching competence and role performance (Singh, 1985).

Sharma (1972) found that narrow questions as compared to open questions were more effective with respect to pupil attainment in terms of knowledge objectives. On the other hand, Shaida (1976) found that the teaching pattern of narrow questions with feedback was significantly effective is the development of knowledge and relation as compared to narrow questions with no feedback. Singh

(1983) reported that Programmed Instruction, and Bloom's Mastery Learning Strategy Influenced Achievement Motivation more that the Conventional Method of Training.

While comparing the Concept Attainment Model and Advance Organizer Model with traditional methods in terms of performance on the concept knowledge test, Chitriv (1983) found that the Advance Organizer Model as well as the Concept Attainment Model were significantly superior to the traditional method, whereas the Advance Organizer Model was superior to the Concept Attainment Model for teaching mathematical concepts to XI grade students. Prose-passage type and pictorial type advance organisers facilitated the retention of Life Science subject matter even after an interval of four weeks (Ghosh, 1986). He also observed that instructional strategy with a pictorial types of advance organiser was found to be better than the prose-passage type of advance organiser. Pandya (1986) reported that both the Advance Organiser Model and Inquiry Training Model were significantly superior to the traditional method in terms of pupil achievement, whereas all the three were equally effective in terms of pupils attitude towards social studies.

The Advance Organizer Model and Operant Conditioning Model were significantly superior to the traditional method in terms of achievement of B.Ed. students in educational psychology (Buddisagar, 1987). The Concept Attainment Model and Biological Science Inquiry Model were found to be significantly superior to conventional teaching in terms of class VIII pupils achievement (Sushma, 1987). The Concept Attainment Model and Inductive Thinking Model were found to be superior to the traditional method in terms of concept attainment and retention (Baveja, 1988).

Programmed learning (Based on Operant Conditioning Model) material has been compared with conventional methods of teaching (Shah, 1964; Desai, 1966; Sharma, 1966; Shah, 1969; Kulkarni, 1969; SIE Gujarat, 1970; Nagar, 1971; Sharma, 1971; Sharma, 1972; Joshi, 1972; Mehta, 1973; Pandya, 1974; Reddy, 1975; Patel, 1975; Govinda, 1976; Chandrakala, 1976; Sabharwal, 1978; Parlikar, 1979; Pandey, 1980; Inamdar, 1981; Suthar, 1981). All these studies reported that programmed learning material was significantly superior to conventional methods of teaching in terms of achievement.

Passi, Singh and Sansanwal (1985) developed a training strategy for training teacher educators in Models of Teaching. The training comprised orientation in the theory of the model, lesson plan guide, teaching analysis guide through lectures and discussion. This was followed by demonstration lessons and practice in quadro. The training strategy was found to be effective in terms of theoretical understanding of the model and a favorable change in teacher educator's reactions towards models of teaching. In this study, the Concept Attainment and Inquiry Training Models were taken up. This strategy was replicated on a different sample of teacher education in 1986. The models of teaching considered were the Advance Organizer Model and the Jurisprudential Inquiry Model. A national project related to value clarification was completed in March, 1988. In this project, the Value Discussion Model and Jurisprudential Inquiry Model were studied. This project was completed by the Department of Education, Devi Ahilya Vishwavidyalaya, Indore, in collaboration with the Department of Teacher Education, Special Education and Extension services, NCERT Again in 1988, a new batch of teacher educators were trained in the Value Analysis Model for studying its impact on the value clarification ability of student-teachers. New models of teaching are being investigated, new indigenous training approaches have been designed. The Ph.D. study related to training has been by Awasthi (1988) who found that the Continuous Demonstration with Pair Practice (CDP) strategy and Intermittent Demonstration with the Quadro Practice (IDP) strategy were found to be equally effective in terms of theoretical understanding of the Concept Attainment Model, while in terms of teaching competency, the IDP-Practice Strategy was significantly superior to the CDP-Practice Strategy.

On the basis of studies presented in this category, it may be said that the conventional method of teaching different subjects at various levels was found to be less effective than various innovative teaching patterns like programmed instruction, instructional strategy and models of teaching in terms of achievement of students. In spite of this, it is difficult to determine which instructional strategy, pattern of teaching, or model of teaching is most appropriate for teaching different subject at various levels. This is due to the fact that no two studies are alike in all respest such as, design, sample, tools, treatment, dependent variables, etc. The researchers took achievement as a criterion variable. There is need to deviate from this traditional approach to selecting a criterion variable. In the case of some studies, the criterion variable belongs to the effective domain. The psychomotor seems to be out of right of researchers. Thus, studies may be designed in developing tools to measure their effects and thus facilitate study of the effectiveness of the model of teaching in terms of instructional and nurtutant effects.

Gupta *et al.* (1992) studied the impact of teaching kit on the trainees and concluded that the teaching kits need to be given place of primary important in the block teaching practice programme in B.Ed. Training. The study revealed that it was possible to use the components of teaching kit at different stages of teaching for all trainees irrespective of their more additions to the contents of the kit (*e.g.* audio cassettes, slides etc.). It can be very useful device for developing the confidence and in building up the morale of teachers undergoing training besides providing them valuable help at different stages of the classroom teaching.

Sharma and Kumar (1993) conducted a study on the views of 300 secondary school teachers about the relative importance of teaching skills. Fifteen most commonly described teaching skills were retained. The result showed that the teachers considered those skills relatively more important which either promoted maximum student involvement in the teaching learning process or were helpful in accelerating the pace of teaching by compensating for lengthy explanations. On the other hand, the skills regarding the pace of teaching were rated at least important. The skills of promoting pupil participation, using teaching aids and questioning, were thus judged as the most important teaching skills.

Agrawal (1994) studied effectiveness of secondary schools teachers in relations to their participation in their own children's academic activities she concluded that if the teacher has insight into the importance of parents' academic participation, he may utilise this in performing his task more effectively. Reduction in unfavourable and negative parental participation lead teacher effectiveness, for enriching his teaching behaviour. The teacher-educators might include "Parental participation in academic activities" as an integral part of teachers' training programme. It was evident that the teachers who were better parenting performed better in their profession too. Thus, it was suggested that the course of B.Ed. training programme should be supplemented with the specific knowledge of parenting.

Gupta *et.at.* (1995) in the documentation of training practices in Western Region of India, under DPEP, reported some innovative practices. Under Shikshak Samakhya Pariyojna (Teachers Empowerment Project) in M.P. he found that every individual teacher was responsible for teaching/learning environment of his/her classroom. Teachers had the potential to make schools beautiful and learning interesting; they got highly motivated if they all involved in decision-making for their training and teaching. If they prepared and used their own teaching. If they prepared and used their own teaching learning material (TLM) they developed greater confidence in themselves, and gained recognition from their peers, their students and local community. Peer support and awareness of new ideas are important for the profession. Practising, successful and the enthusiastic teachers were the best people to train their fellow teachers. There was a culture of co-sharing, co-working and co-learning with better inter-departmental co-ordination. The methodology of training at DIET's in M.P. were found lecture method, workshop method, demonstration method, lecture-cum-demonstration method, group discussion, excursion teaching method with emphasis on learner-centered approach, school readiness programme, playway method, activity based learning, practical work, development of low cost teaching aids, achieving M.L.L., competency based teaching and value education.

The Methodology of training in the Inservice Training Practice in Goa (Gupta *et.al.* 1995) includes objectives based activities, participatory approach of training, micro level study pattern, use of local resources, stress on situational learning objectives based evaluation, stress on basics of learning providing out of classroom learning situations also. In the in-service teachers training programme by CERT Gujarat training programme was constantly improved in the light of feedback. The mode of training was also modified. There was provision of reorientation of the participants for the difficult concept on the basis of teachers' feedback.

The Advance Organiser Model (AOM) was found to be effective in developing teaching competence among student-teachers under simulated as well as classroom conditions (Gupta, 1991). While Kaushik (1988) studied the long-term effect of advance organisers in relation to reading ability, intelligence and scientific attitude of the learners and found that the general introduction or an overview, which generally precedes learning material, is less effective as compared to the advance organisers. Secondly, the benefit derived from advance organisers is positively correlated with higher intelligence, reading comprehension and scientific attitude.

Chaudhury (1989) investigated and found that the teaching skills and competence developed among student-teachers through the use of Concept Attainment Model (CAM) are easily transferable in other teaching situations, besides the teaching of concepts, this study recommended the use of CAM instead of spending much time on the Micro-teaching Technique to develop teaching skills.

Mahajan (1992) found that during the peer group sessions as well as classroom teaching sessions, the group taught by CAM was found to be superior to the groups taught by AOM as well as the routine method as far as the teaching ability of student-teachers was concerned.

An elaborate three phase experimental study of CAM and ITM (Inquiry Training Model) was conducted by Passi, Singh and Sansanwal (1991) to find the efficacy of the training strategy adopted for training application in Indian classroom application. It brought about significant favourable changes in the attitudes of both teacher educators and the student-teachers towards the models.

Malhara (1988) compared the effectiveness of competition oriented and co-operation-oriented methods of teaching and found that cooperative methods of teaching were more effective than the methods of competitive teaching in developing various skills and creative faculties.

Joshi and Kumar (1983) studied the effect of the skill-based approach and decision-making ability on developing the teaching competence in teacher-trainees. It was found that a gradual increase in the number of skills, time duration and pupil number resulted in higher teaching competence as compared to all the skills being taken together. Atrya (1989) concluded that teaching effectiveness was significantly correlated with values and job satisfaction.

Basi (1991) examined teaching competence of language teachers in relation to job satisfaction, locus of control and professional burn-out. Singh (1988) attempted to establish a relationship between teaching efficiency and job satisfaction as also with socio-economic status and found a positive relationship.

Teaching attitude and achievement had bearing on teaching efficiency. Bhasin (1988) found a positive correlation between attitude towards teaching and teaching efficiency. Kukreti (1992) attempted to find the psychological correlates of teaching efficiency and More (1988) worked on personality correlates of teaching efficiency. Shah (1991) examined the predictive value of the determinants of teaching efficiency.

Nautiyal (1992) examined teaching in relation to morale, values and student's perception of teacher characteristics. Principals' effectiveness has also been studied by Usmani (1988) in relation to professional attainment, socio-economic background, values and attitude towards teaching.

Dwelling in the field of Micro-teaching Sultana (1988) established the superiority of Micro-teaching in bringing about changes in behaviour of student-teachers of science between the first and fifth teaching sessions. Singh (1987) arrived at the conclusion that remedial instructional Micro-teaching was effective in improving the skills of probing questioning and demonstration of both more and less experienced primary school teachers.

Singh (1988) used Flanders Interaction Analysis Category System for observing teachers' classroom behaviour and attempted to predict it form attitudes (Measured by the Minnesota Teacher Attitude Inventory). The findings of the study revealed that there was a significant relationship between attitude towards teaching and classroom verbal interaction of student teachers of secondary level. Indirect influence, pupil talk, pupil initiation ratio, are positively related to attitude towards teaching in both male and female groups. Lecturing, Criticising, Justifying authority, direct influence and destructiveness are negatively correlated with attitude towards teaching.

For teacher education at secondary stage 'Curriculum Framework for Quality Teacher Education' (NCTE, 1998) recommends, apart from theory, practice teaching in schools and practical work, pedagogical analysis of two school teaching subjects, observation of model lessons, Internship and School Experiences. It further states:

> Pre-requisite to preparing a prospective teacher can be thought of providing certain inputs such as induction programme, exposure to school experiences with special focus on educational environment of the school,.........observation of classroom teaching and related activities. Induction programme might include acquainting the intending teachers with the school settings, the school programmes curricular and co-curricular. In addition, they will be prepared for actual classroom teaching and the roles they are expected to assume during the course of practice teaching/internship by way of focussed discussions, demonstration lessons, preparation of lesson plans so as to encompass teaching for cognitive, affective and psychomotor development.
>
> Practice teaching is essentially a joint responsibility of teacher training institution and the school involving teacher educators, prospective teachers and school teachers. Teacher educators will help in facilitating and guiding the activities as implied by the pre-instructional, instructional and post-instructional phase through which a student teacher has to progress. The role of a school teacher in this joint effort lies in extending co-operation to the teacher educator and the intending teacher. Various aspects, as referred to above, will have to be suitably adapted to varying structures and designs of teacher education.
>
> Efforts need to be directed towards developing in the teacher trainee certain competencies and skills which would be helpful in the shaping of the teacher for an effective role play. It is essentially directed towards capacity building which may

embrace, among other competencies, managerial skills, organisational efficiency, leadership skills, democratic attitudes, innovative and creative abilities.

The teachers' role, which they will be required to play in the school situation other than classroom teaching, may extend to a variety of activities, such as maintenance of school records and registers, management of laboratories and library, preparation, repair and selection of instructional aids and equipments, selection and preparation of textual materials, preparation of tests and assignments, admission and selection of students, maintenance of progress reports of students, preparation of school budget and development plans, beautification of school and classroom management etc. The institutional activities within the school environs may include dramatic clubs, stage activities, literary activities, inter-house activities and sports and games, organisation of educational tours etc." (NCTE, 1998).

Apart from these "Student-teachers may undertake a case study of a school (generally a practising school) for identifying its strengths and weaknesses, needs and problems, specific learning problems, such as drop-outs, drug abuse, behavioural problems, learning difficulties etc".

On the duration of B.Ed. programme the NCTE document clearly states, "Through the national consultations initiated by the NCTE, a strong consensus emerged in favour of enhancing the duration of B.Ed. programme from one year to two years". The practice teaching will, thus, require through preparation, detailed supervision and adequate time. Its gain would, obviously, be acquisition of higher level of teaching competencies. Internship programme shall be enriched to provide all the experience that a teacher needs. After completion of the period of internship, the prospective teacher will acquire necessary experiences for working in school...... The implementation of internship will also need increased duration (NCTE, 1998).

2.6 The Changing Context of Teacher Education

At the threshold of the last decade of the twentieth century, economic, social and cultural changes are accelerating exponentially. These changes are often linked to the continuous process of scientific and technological development. Education in many countries is responding to these changes, incorporating educational developments and reforms. Reform in teacher education constitutes part of the reform movement in education. Most countries have recognised the importance of pre-service education for teachers. There are a number of developments in this area, the major ones are described here briefly.

2.6.1 Frameworks for Teacher Education Pedagogy

We can identify following major orientations to teacher education that have substantial implications for the design and/or selection of teacher education pedagogies. These include (i) a practical/craft orientation, (ii) a technological orientation, (iii) a personal orientation, (iv) an academic orientation, and (v) a critical/social orientation. Each of these orientations reflects some what different stance towards the goals and nature of teacher preparation. We are currently in the midst of a profound shift in the core conceptions of teaching and teacher education, one that is transforming basic notions in the field. This shift is reflected and then addressed on the emerging conception of teachers as reflective professionals.

2.6.1.1 The Practical /Craft Orientation

From a practical/craft perspective, emphasis in teacher education is on preparing teachers to deal effectively with the "real world" of schooling – the management of classes, the conduct of lessons, and the performance of many other tasks a teacher faces throughout the school year. Of course, the teaching methods to be used or the models to be emulated may well represent the latest advances in teaching, however, the stress is not just on theory but rather on practical ways of carrying out these approaches. This orientation fosters an interest in demonstration lessons, exemplary models, and apprenticeships with especially competent and committed practitioners.

Practically, craft knowledge, and apprenticeship in teacher education have often been seen as unscientific and conservative against the promise of professionalisation, innovation, and reform arising from psychological research or philosophical premises (Buchmann, 1987). Recently, however, cognitive scientists extolled the virtue of situated cognition, communities of practice, and apprenticeship modes of learning (Brown, Collins, and Duguid, 1989). Moreover the craft perspective has been given new energy within and emerging focus on the special knowledge or "wisdom" teachers derive from the actual practice of teaching and from examining and reflecting on their own experiences (Gimmett and Makinnon, 1992).

2.6.1.2 The Technological Orientation

The technological perspective in teacher education has roots in behavioural psychology and the associated procedures of task analysis and instructional design, exemplified, for instance, in programmed instruction. From this perspective, teaching competence is a composite of discrete skills, especially skills that have been shown to be associated with high student achievement, and teacher education is process of skill training (Gliessman, 1984). The most renowned version of this approach went under the name of Performance (or Competency) Based Teacher Education (Gage and Winne, 1975).

Pedagogies that are especially capatible with this orientation include laboratory skill training methods (for example, Micro-teaching and mini courses), intensive observation and feedback strategies, peer coaching, and training-oriented simulations. (Cruickshank and Metcalf, 1990).

Technologists sometimes have skeptical attitude toward field experiences and apprenticeships in conventional classrooms because these experiences foster a survival mentality and often train prospective teachers in traditional practices rather than research-based skills. They occasionally argue, therefore, that laboratory training experiences can serve as substitutes for field observations and even student teaching (Smith, Cohen, and Pearl, 1969).

With the emphasis on thinking, reflection and decision-making in teacher preparation, this area of teacher education pedagogy is undergoing a fundamental reappraisal (Zumwalt, 1982).

2.6.1.3 The Personal Orientation

Perhaps the most vigorous line of work in teacher education today in U.S.A. is that focussed on teacher's personal knowledge and stories (Carter, 1993; Elbaz, 1991; Goodson, 1992). Here the focus often ranges beyond the immediately technical issues of curriculum and classroom lessons to encompass teachers' biographies. Thus, teaching events are framed within a context of a teacher's life history or narrative. As a result, the central themes are often moral and philosophical having more to do with feelings, purposes, images, aspirations, and personal meanings than with teaching skills or method in isolation from personal experience or biography. For an individual teacher, theory and practice are integrated through her or his narrative unity of experience (Connelly and Clandinin, 1990).

Traditionally, personalized teacher education rested on pedagogies derived from counselling, such as interviews with a caring person, support groups, journals, and the like. The modern emphasis on personal knowledge has expanded these pedagogies to include opportunities for reflection, the study and writing of stories and cases, action research, and the like (Carr and Kemmis, 1986; Rusell and Munby, 1992).

2.6.1.4 The Academic Orientation

An emphasis on solid preparation in the core academic disciplines of the university curriculum has always been strong, especially among faculty in the liberal arts and sciences (Bestor, 1953). Proponents of this position are particularly wary of the substance and rigor of pedagogical courses offered in education departments. They prefer rather that teachers be educated through a rigorous programme of academic preparation followed by apprenticeship with a skilled and academically prepared teacher. Subject matter preparation is certainly at the heart of the teacher education agenda today. It is a central theme in the influential report of the Holmes Group (1986) on teacher education reform, and it is the focus of substantial research programmes on pedagogical content knowledge (Grossman,1990; Gudmundsdottir, 1991) and subject matter teaching (Ball and McDiarmid, 1990). There is a distinct emphasis in this emerging area on the use of cases as exemplars for teacher preparation.

2.6.1.5 The Critical/Social Orientation

Central to this point is the notion of teacher empowerment; that is the essential role of teachers as owners of their knowledge and their destinies (Garrison, 1988). There is an emphasis on teachers' personal understanding of a situation and their own purposes, values and associations. The emphasis in teacher education is on the process that simulates personal reflection, such as action research (Carr and Kemmis, 1986) of life histories (Woods, 1987), methods that start from a teacher's own understandings and construction of meaning.

2.6.2 Emerging Conceptions of Reflective Professional

Implicit in this survey of orientation is a fundamental change in the conceptual underpinnings of teacher education. On several fronts, there is an emerging cognizance of the essential role of teacher's reflective capacities of observation, analysis, interpretation and decision-making in professional practice (Russell and Munby, 1992; Zeichner and Liston, 1987). The emphasis is on teachers' ability to inquire into teaching and think critically about their work using their craft and personal knowledge as well as the knowledge derived from studies of learning, development and society.

This array of assumptions of commitments, reflecting cognitive, personal, and constructivist ancestry, has underscored narrative, dialogue, and inquiry in the preparation of teachers.

2.6.3. Teaching Laboratories and Simulations

Laboratory training methods, which began to flourish in the 1960s, were hailed as the harbinger of professionalization in teaching because they placed teacher preparation on a solid scientific, technological, and practical base (Allen and Ryan, 1969). The convergence of scientific and technical ideas gave rise to three somewhat distinct traditions: (i) Observations and feedback strategies, (ii) Laboratory skill training designs, and (iii) Simulations (Cruickshank and Metcalf, 1990).

Drawing on reviews (Copeland, 1982; Cruickshank and Metcalf, 1990) it is possible to formulate the following general conclusions about laboratory skill training in teacher education:

(1) Novice (and a sometime experienced) teachers acquire the target skills of a training laboratory. Most studies also indicate that considerable improvement in performance is apparent in the second round of teaching.

(2) Some evidence suggests that learning what a teaching skill actually is and how to recognise it in operation is a key ingredient of laboratory training. Wagner (1973), for instance, found that cognitive discrimination training (Learning to recognise the skill in protocol materials) was as effective as Micro-teaching in acquisition of a teaching skill. This had led to an emphasis on concept teaching and cognition in laboratories pedagogies (Gliessman and Pugh, 1987).

(3) Transfer of teaching skills from the laboratory to the classroom problem has underscored the importance of coaching and other strategies to bridge the distance between the laboratory and the classroom (Joyce and Showers, 1981).

(4) Teaching laboratories remain a popular component of many teacher education programme.

2.6.3.1 Simulation

In the past few years, there has been considerable interest in the development of teaching simulations for use in the clinical preparation of teachers. Brown and Gliessman (1987), for example, developed a programme at Indiana University that used interactive video to train teachers to identify instances of need, achievement, sociometric status, and scholastic ability among pupils in brief videotaped classroom segments. The emphasis in this programme was largely on concept formation, labelling and problem solving by proposing solutions to problems depicted in the video taped scenes.

A skill training model underlies the simulation in which an IBM PC with separate monitor displays to train teachers in giving feedback for correct and incorrect answers and to adjust the pace of question asking during lessons (Strang, Landrum, and Lynch, 1989).

An alternative to this emphasis on skill training has begun to emerge in teacher education and is changing the intellectual context for the development of simulations in the field. In this alternative view, teaching is seen not as skill enactment but as situated cognition (Brown, Collins, and Duguid, 1989). Teaching in other words, is seen to involve processes of recognition, comprehension, and problem solving in a complex social environment characterized by multi-dimensionality, unpredictability, and immediacy.

2.6.4 Field-Based Pedagogies

In keeping with the long tradition of apprenticeship in learning to teach, field experiences have been a central ingredient in teacher preparation for many years. Recently, however, their use has expanded in both the number of occasions offered during teacher education and the amount of time devoted to such events (Guyton and McIntyre, 1990). More over, recent advances in our understanding of classroom knowledge (Carter and Doyle, 1987), case methods (Sykes and Bird, 1992), practical arguments (Fenstermacher and Richardson, 1993), reflection (Russell and

Munby, 1992), and the process of learning to teach (Carter, 1990) have contributed to a reformulation of conceptions of the role of field experiences in becoming a teacher. As a result, considerable energy is being directed to creating and elaborating the pedagogical aspects of field experiences.

2.6.4.1 Learning from Experience

Field experience have traditionally reflected a practical/craft orientation to teacher preparation. By spending time in the field, candidates for teaching learn what the "real world" of teaching is all about, are able to watch models of exemplary practice, can tap the practical wisdom of experienced professionals, and in a variety of other ways begin their apprenticeship in teaching.

2.6.4.2 Observation Guides

Novice teachers may benefit from guidance in how to observe teaching. Typically, this guidance is provided through observation schedules or guides that students take with them to the field and complete during or immediately after their observations.

The development of observation guides received considerable technical impetus from the work on interaction analysis (Flanders, 1970) and the vast number of similar efforts to devise systematic observational tools for the study of teaching (Evertson and Green, 1986). These category systems were extolled for their objectivity, scientific precision, and analytical rigor, and numerous studies were conducted to ascertain their impact on novice teachers' performance (Cruickshank and Metcalf, 1990). These instruments also provided a common language for talking about teaching and thus in some situations helped to promote an analytical perspective among candidates and to the filed observations more closely to the content of perparation programmes.

2.6.4.3 Structured Assignments

The complexity of field experience is also reduced frequently through the use of assignments designed to enable novices to practice parts of the total array of teaching responsibilities. Thus, candidates are often asked to assist the regular teacher in distributing supplies or grading papers, to tutor individual students or teach brief lessons to small groups, and the like. Such structured experiences are recommended for their practicality in introducing teacher education students to teaching responsibilities and for providing a common basis for discussions about teaching.

2.6.4.4 Opportunities to Write about Teaching

Journal writing appears to be a mainstay in reports of practices that promote reflection in teacher thinking (Bolin, 1988; Knowles and Holt-Reynolds, 1991; Rovegno, 1992; Tabchnick and Ziechner, 1984; Zeichner and Liston, 1987). Rovegno (1992) reports that students wrote in "dialogue journals, reflecting on their progress toward becoming effective teachers". Journals also provide students with opportunities to "vent frustrations, express enthusiasm for teaching, cope with the pain of leaving students, and reflect on all the complex dimensions of preservice development" (Zulich, Bean, and Herrick, 1991), as well as revealing "many of the catalysts and inhibitors in prospective teachers' past and contemporary experiences, and in their thinking about future practices" (Knowles and Holt- Reynolds, 1991).

Bolin (1988) recommends that teacher educators respond to journal entries by asking questions and commenting on the content of the writing, thus providing opportunities for the teacher educators to uncover uncertainty in students' thinking or locate events that cause dissonance. Bolin also argues that journals provide " a useful tool in the guiding (students) and assessing the extent to which [they] have become more deliberative teachers". Zeichner and Liston (1987) state that journals provide information to the supervisors about the context of the students' field experiences as well as a picture of the students' development as teachers. For the teacher education students, Tabachnick and Zeichner (1984) report that journals enabled clarification of perspectives and the adoption of a "reflective or analytic stance toward teaching practice".

Carter (1994) has devised a writing task involving well remembered events that is especially suited to helping novices learn from field experiences. A well remembered event is an incident or episode that a student observes in a school situation and considers, for his or her own reasons, especially salient. In exploratory studies, Carter (1994) and Carter and Gnzalez (1993) obtained preliminary evidence that these well-remembered events provide a window to the cognitive world of teaching and to the acquisition of teachers' event knowledge of classrooms.

A variety of "life history" methods have emerged recently that consist of having teacher education students write autobiographical accounts (Crow, 1987; Goodson, 1992; Knowles, 1992; Woods, 1987). These personal stories are grounded in the notion of narrative unity—that is, the coherence and continuity of an individual's experience.

2.6.4.5 Seminars and Conversations

Another practice that appears prominently in writing about field experiences is dialogue. Bolin (1988) notes that journals furnish opportunities for students to talk with each other about their experiences, whether through a "roving" journal or in a seminar setting. Rovegno (1992) recommends on-campus class discussions about observations as well as individual conferences with the teacher educators. Killian and McIntyre (1988) suggest placements that offer multiple opportunities for students of teaching to talk with their co-operating teachers. Applegate and Lasley (1982), Tabachnick and Zeichner (1984), and Zeichner and Liston (1987) all advocate weekly seminars that provide opportunities for students, co-operating teachers, and university faculty (in some combination) to reflect about experiences through conversations. The seminars have the potential to expose misconceptions, fears, and frustrations from all participants, as well as offer opportunities to celebrate successes (MacKinnon and Grunau, 1991). Pulling together students from several classrooms within a school allows for "the plurality of vision that is essential to a more comprehensive understanding" of classroom processes (Elbaz, 1988).

Supervision would seem to provide an ideal setting for conversations about teaching, but is most often discussed in relation to student teaching rather than early field experiences (Glickman and Bey, 1990).

One innovative and theoretically grounded pedagogy developed by Fenstermacher and Richardson (1993) involves the elicitation of "practical arguments." The premises upon which teachers ground their decisions about which actions to take to achieve particular circumstances.

2.6.5 Cases and Case Methods

Cases and case methods have been a customary part of clinical teaching in the professions of medicine, law architecture, and business for most of this century (Carter and Unklesbay, 1989; Doyle, 1990). In the past few years, however there has been a massive increase in enthusiasm for cases and case methods in the education of teachers (Merseth, 1991; Sykes and Bird, 1992). As a result several casebooks and collections on case methods have recently appeared and a rich array of cases, ranging from short episodes to lengthy descriptions of year long experiences and form general teaching dilemmas to subject specific reasoning, are now readily available to teacher educators (Hinely and Ford, 1994; Greenwood and Parkay, 1989; Kowalski, Weaver, and Hensen, 1990; Shulman and Cobert, 1987, 1988; Silverman, Welty, and Lyon, 1991).

The overall goal of using cases as precedents is two-fold: (1) to help student acquire the situated knowledge of teaching they need in order to "think like a teacher" (Kleinfeld, 1992), and (2) to engender habits of analysis inquiry, and reflection that will empower them to continue to grow in their professional understandings and abilities. There is also some evidence to suggest that learning from cases is especially suited to the development of cognitive flexibility and the acquisition of knowledge in ill-structured domains (Spiro and others, 1987).

Beyond the enthusiasm for cases as occasions for clinical reasoning, there is an emerging sense that cases capture the essentially storied nature of teacher's knowledge (Carte, 1993). This view of cases as stories reflects a conviction that narrative is not only a powerful pedagogical tool for representing teaching but also a means of capturing the concerns and motivations of novice teachers and helping them acquire understandings and dispositions that reflect the fundamental way in which teachers, regardless of their experiences, know and think about their work (Carter, 1993; Clandinin, 1992); Gudmundsdottier, 1991; Elbaz, 1991).

2.6.6 Cognitive Apprenticeship

The concept of cognitive apprenticeship adapts the features of traditional apprenticeship to the teaching and learning of cognitive skills in schools (Collins, Brown, and Holum, 1991). While the traditional form of apprenticeship may be applicable to the development of technical expertise and the applicable to the development of technical expertise and the application of principles and concepts, the development of critical analytic expertise and the skills of deliberate action will require a learning approach that can uncover the thinking of expert teachers and make it visible to the learning practitioner.

The most important difference between a traditional apprenticeship and a cognitive apprenticeship is that in a cognitive apprenticeship the thinking processes of the teacher and the learner must be made visible. Cognitive research identifying cognitive and metacognitive processes is making this possible. A second difference is the need to situate cognitive tasks in contexts that make sense to students. In a traditional apprenticeship, they are already so situated.

There are several instructional strategies that are effective in uncovering thinking process. They include reciprocal teaching, small problem-solving groups, class demonstrations, control strategies to direct student learning tasks, and post-mortem analyses. Professional practice schools are being designed to support this kind of learning. For example, clustering of student teachers within the professional practice school provides the opportunity for observation and interaction with other learners. Some professional practice schools are pairing student teachers in one classroom or with teams of teachers (Lemlech and Fliart, 1992). This encourages reciprocal teaching, one strategy in a cognitive apprenticeship. Professional practice schools, by design, encourage groups of teachers to share responsibility for student teachers.

2.6.7 Professional Development Schools

Moving teacher preparation programmes into professional development schools has begun to change teacher education in the United States (Goodlad, 1993; Winitski, Stoddard, & O'Keefe, 1992). Conventional teacher preparation programmes introduce prospective teachers to current theory and practice in a series of campus-based courses, followed by an intensive experience in practice teaching. In contrast, teacher preparation course in professional development schools (PDS) offer new and veteran teachers opportunities to test theoretical constructs from preparatory classes against the daily press of work with students (Stallings, 1991). The purpose of collaboration in a professional development school is to improve practice among both new and seasoned teachers, lending force and coherence to local school improvement plans and creating a center for the development of knowledge for the teaching profession. A professional development school creates a setting in which universities and schools share in the preparation of new teachers and where mutual renewal is a shared goal (Goodlad, 1993). Simply transplanting university courses to the schools does little to improve practice in either setting. To support reform teacher education faculty must redesign their courses to support on-going experimentation in a setting that becomes inherently unstable as change takes hold.

Local conditions vary, but the central principle remains the same :

> *If teachers are consistently supported over time in a way that will allow them to develop and grow as they teach, they will gradually professionalize themselves* (Leo-Nyquist, 1990).

Three recent adaptations to the pre-existing campus-based

programme have allowed teacher preparation courses conducted in professional development schools to support school and professional renewal simultaneously :

Integrated Practica : Each Secondary Education course includes a practicum in which interns test educational theory in practice and in which continuous testing forces personal theories to evolve.

Result Orientation : Each course requires students to make something happen in the life of the school, to use what they are learning to make a difference among students and teachers.

Professional Portfolios : Each course requires students to assemble evidence that they can contribute to student learning and school change (Dollase, 1996). Teaching interns must demonstrate mastery of learning from the teachers preparation curriculum in a school with its own unique character and evolving sense of purpose.

While school-based interns are completing their first teaching licensure requirements, teams of professional teachers in a PDS are involved in a school development course, conducting research over a full school year in support of school improvement (Clarke *et al.*, in press). The simultaneous activity of preservice interns pursuing practicum assignments for their courses and professional teachers working together on problem-solving teams creates an enriched development setting that fosters adaptive growth.

University students establish tutoring centres, work as assistants in team-taught high school classes, correct papers, package learning materials for unit plans, and join in special events. High school teachers assume increasing importance in preparing the new teachers, conducting seminars, supervising interns and eventually teaching courses in the established curriculum. The functions of the PDS are three-fold : to serve as field placement site for teacher candidates, to promote the professional development of experienced teachers, and to advance the knowledge base on teaching and learning by supporting reflection, inquiry, and research. Stallings, Bossung, and Martin (1990) compared student-teachers placed in PDSs with those placed in conventional settings. Forty-four candidates in the Houston Teaching Academy (an inner-city PDS) were compared with twenty-five control student teachers placed in middle-class, multicultural settings, both urban and sub-urban. A key element of this particular PDS programme was a weekly seminar: student teachers met with their university supervisor for forty-five minutes and then were joined by the co-operating teachers. Multiple data sources were used to assess the effectiveness of the PDS experience : observations, questionnaires, interviews, journals. Based on the observational data, PDS candidates outperformed controls on questioning, praise and support, per cent of students on task, and per cent of academic statements. Follow-up studies (Stallings, 1992) revealed that many graduates of this inner-city PDS programme had obtained employment in multiracial schools and were happy in these positions.

The professional development school concept and the "whole school approach" to field experiences, both enjoying recent popularity, hold particular promise as well. Studies of various professional development school models (for example, Clarke and La Londe, 1992; Mc Nay and Cole, 1993; Stallings and Kowalski, 1990; Winitzky, Stoddard, and O'Keefe, 1992) highlight opportunities for preservice teachers to develop affinity, affiliation, and professional identity; to get a better sense of the complexities of schools, teaching, and being a teacher; to "come close" to the realities of teaching; and to develop a more solid foundation for on going development.

3

THE PROSPECTIVE MODEL OF TEACHER EDUCATION

In the newest wave of calls for educational reform, many teacher education faculties are changing the structure of their programmes. Some are making substantive changes as well. It is important that teacher education programmes be coherent courses of study tied to what teachers need to know and what teachers need to be able to do in a society that is an information technology society and that is global and diverse. Thus, there is an increasing demand today for teacher education programmes to articulate their respective knowledge bases and the philosophical assumptions on which those knowledge bases are founded.

The reforms of the nineteenth century that resulted from the rise of science and the notion of the malleability of humankind and society changed the educational system significantly. But once again, as we enter the twenty-first century, demands on the educatinal system have changed dramatically. Today our schools must serve an information technology, must take a more global perspective, and must meet the needs of all students from diverse cultures.

3.1 Traditional and Progressive Strands

Both the structure and the substance of teacher education

programmes are related to the philosophical assumptions on which the various movements and counter-movements in education are built. 'Me The traditional approach has as its aim the transmission of the culture. Its philosophical foundations are in Pláto and Aristotle, in the dualistic notions of pre-scientific theocracy and faculty psychology and a belief in the permanence of Truth.

The term progressive, when applied to education, has been used by writers in various ways. Some use the term to describe the movement that saw people as creators of their culture, knowledge as emergent, the movement that dominated the progressive era of Dewey and others who were putting the pragmatist philosophy into educational terms in the early part of the twentieth century. Others use the term to categorise the various reforms movements of the late nineteenth century, which were reactions to the traditional approach to education. The term progressive movement is used to refer to those reforms with their foundation in the late nineteenth century that were a result of the rise of science and the child study movement, the beginnings of the study of education as a science, the constructionist approach to knowledge, and the recognition of the malleability of humans and society with the concomitant notion that one of the aims of education should be the transformations of the society. The reforms are viewed as reactions not so much to traditionalist content but to the way content was delivered in the schools.

The progressive movement essentially created innovation models with a view of the functions of education as creating a better life for all citizens and thus a better democracy for the society. The models of teacher education influenced by the progressive reform movements have as their aim not only the transmission of the culture in a set of permanent truths but also the construction of new truth and the transmission of that part of the culture that will enable the society to transform itself, to make a better society for a more and more inclusive society.

In the traditional model of teacher education, which persists today in some programmes, the beginning teacher must know the functions to be performed in the classroom, know that content of subjects to be handed down to students, and be trained in predetermined skills to teach that knowledge.

The rise of science and the conceptualisation of humankind and society as malleable, not predetermined, gave rise to four liberal reform movements in the late nineteenth century. The four major reform movements have been characterized as (1) the humanist movement with its ideal for a liberal education for all and the importance of a common curriculum, (2) the developmentalist movement with its emphasis on looking to the stages of development in the child to determine what should be taught, (3) the social efficiency movements, which focussed on examining teaching behaviours that bring results, and (4) the social melioration movement with its ideal of using the school to reconstruct society.

3.2 Academic Approach

The academic approach to teacher education is an influence of the humanist movement. For the humanists of the nineteenth century, the development of reasoning power was the central function of the schools and that was best accomplished through the study of five basic liberal arts and by learning and applying the skills of accurate observation, correct recording, classification, categorisation, and correct inferences. In the academic approach to teacher education, the child is viewed as a developing scholar and the teacher is to be trained to think like a scholar and practice the disciplines with children. The knowledge base is in the core disciplines of the liberal arts and sciences.

For some, the professional component in this approach comes from a constructionist point of view and would focus on teachers knowing the cognitive process involved in learning and the structures of the discipline. Knowledge of subject matter is just one focus of teacher education, representation and translation of subject matter knowledge to promote student understanding being a very important second focus.

3.3 Personalistic Approach

The developmentalist or personalistic approach to teacher education grew out of the child study movement initiated by Stanley Hall and others as an outgrowth of the new status of science in the nineteenth century. The developmentalist approach focuses on the stages of development of the child. Proponents of this model have a view of humanity influenced by Rousseau, Froebel, Horace Mann, and the notion that the natural order of development in the child is the most significant and scientifically defensible basis for deciding what should be taught.

Because for the developmentalists education should facilitate the unfolding natural goodness of the child, the aims of education become individual and idiosyncratic, and thus learning outcome standardisation is emphasised. For the teacher, there are no standard competencies to be acquired. The focus is instead on coming to terms with self, acquiring knowledge of the stages of child development, and demonstrating an empathetic relationship with students more as equals than in an authoritarian role. In the personalistic approach to teacher education that developed in the twentieth century, coming to terms with oneself in the knowledge base for teachers includes clarifying one's values and discovering one's personal meaning and style in teaching.

3.4 Competency Approach

The competency or outcomes-based approaches to teacher education originated in the social efficiency movement whose advocates at the turn of the century shared the developmentalists' view that the key to successful education lay in scientific data on the child. But these approaches began to focus on the study of teaching activities and moved ultimately to notions about application of scientific management techniques successful in increasing efficiency in industry. The competency approach is an industrial model of education, with a mechanistic view of the child and of what should be taught. For proponents of the competency and outcomes-based approaches, knowledge is made up of discrete competencies that can be taught and assessed separately. The aim of the social efficiency reformists was standardization and efficiency in the curriculum. Outcomes were specified for the training of teachers, and supervision of teaching activities was considered essential. The competency orientation to teacher education developed in the 1960s and 1970s was the culmination of the development of various interaction analysis systems.

3.5 Social Reconstructionist Approach

In the social reconstructionist or reconceptualist approach to teacher education, school settings are seen as uncertain, dynamic, and problematic. Reconceptualisation is the basis of Zeichner's view of the inquiry model of teacher education that has its roots in the progressive social melioration movement and would seem to be the basis of current attempts in teacher education reform to further professionalise the work of teaching (Zeichner, 1983).

Knowledge is viewed as constructionist a product of thinking rather than something that is static and permanent. The aim of education is to facilitate children in their struggle to become, and to reconstruct the society that, like the individual and knowledge, is constructivist in nature, struggling to become.

The knowledge base for the teacher in the social reconstructionist approach must include awareness of political and social contexts of schooling. Teachers must be prepared to assess classroom actions for their ability to contribute to equity and social justice in school and in society. Thus, problem solving and group dynamics are very important skills, as are those activities that foster the reflective capacities of observation, analysis, critical thinking, and decision-making.

3.6 Synthesis View

The reconceputalistic model addresses the transformation of subject matter, as does the academic model of teacher education. Shulman (1986) also cites the process/product research that would be part of the pedagogical knowledge necessary for teachers and the cognitive development of critical thinking skills of both teachers and students characteristics, respectively, of the competency and developmental approaches to teacher education. Thus, in Shulman's model, rather than rules and prescriptions for classroom application, knowledge and methods of inquiry useful in deliberating about teaching problems and practices are in the knowledge base.

The teacher education faculty that would reflect today on the four common places of schooling the student, the teacher, the subject matter, and the context of schooling would necessarily be influenced by the impact of the four reform movements of the nineteenth century. The child study movement, for instance, changed the view of the child from the soul that must be saved through regimentation and strict discipline to the physical and emotional individual that would construct his or her own knowledge. The social efficiency movement saw the beginnings of the science of teaching with its focus on behaviour, attitudes, and interactions of the teacher. The academic movement forced the focus on subject matter from an emphasis on rote memorization of a fixed body of knowledge to be passively received on the basis of the authority of the teacher to a focus on the transformation of knowledge to fit the cognitive stages of the learner.

3.7 Overview of Teaching Methods

It will be apparent that many teaching methods have a long history. The main changes that have occurred have been rearrangements of existing patterns, the development of new emphases, or, as in more recent times, a more thorough psychological analysis of learning and teaching, and, as a result, a change in the nature and effect of some of the processes used by teachers.

Teaching methods are not random collections of techniques. They fit into a general framework which gives consistency to the teaching processes and provides a reasonable justification for them. The framework or general approach may be built from various elements. Commonly, there may be a theory of learning, a view of the nature of teaching, and a conviction about significant educational goals. In addition, there is inevitably a current mode or view of what is needed at the present time, a kind of educational zeitgeist that determines the favour and thrust of the framework. For a variety of reasons, political, cultural, educational, or even idiosyncratic, an interest in methods may develop that favours a particular point of view at a particular time. It may be conviction that children should be taught to think, or compose speeches, or drilled more thoroughly in basic skills, or taught discipline and obedience, or encouraged to express themselves more effectively, or any of several other considered judgements.

Most teachers throughout history have readily accepted and used the traditional methods by which they were themselves taught. They were habituated to them over the many years of their schooling, and their own scholastic achievements were evidence of the success of such methods. For them to change to a different pattern they must be convinced of the need to change and they must be provided with a feasible alternative or a means of developing one for themselves.

Change in methods of teaching has been an evolutionary movement with little that can be regarded as a substantial or drastic innovation. The more noticeable changes in teaching methods have usually been associated with wider social and cultural changes. Four obvious times of change and the educators associated with modifications in teaching methods have been those of the early Italian Renaissance in which the humanists Guarino and Vittorino played leading parts, the seventeenth-century scientific movement which exercised Comenius's mind. The romantic and re-constructive period of the late eighteenth and early nineteenth century which produced Pestalozzi, Herbart, and Froebel, and the initiation of mass culture in the early years of the twentieth century which stimulated the Progressives and the educators in communist countries.

Each of these persons and groups had perceptive and interesting minds and made significant contributions. Three, Pestalozzi, the Progressives, and the communist educators initiated ideas on method that had a pronounced and immediate effect on modern education. Pestalozzi introduced the notion that teaching methods should be based on a careful psychological analysis of human thinking and demonstrated in practice the kinds of methods that resulted from such an approach. He thereby provided a lead from which Herbart developed a powerful instructional technique and he opened the way for the considerable contribution that educational and cognitive psychologists were to make to the further refinement of teaching processes. The Progressive's innovatory contribution was two-fold. They broke the traditional mould more drastically than had ever been done before, and thus made more feasible the development of new teaching methods suitable to the new societies of the twentieth century. They were also the first to use pupil activity as the central component in teaching and learning. Activity was expressed physically, emotionally, and intellectually. The Progressives, in exploring the connection between action and intellectual development, made wide use of teaching through problem solving, and encouraged creative kinds of expressive activities. They did, in fact, bring a new dimension into teaching. The communist educators concentrated on a particular kind of activity, productive work, and made it a fundamental part of education; but, more significantly, they worked out comprehensive and successful methods of teaching for a widespread new form of society, the collective.

Changes also appear to correspond to major shifts in the way in which teachers view their task. From time to time there is a swing between what might be called an instructional approach and an educational one. When teachers find their main interest to be in the subject matter which they teach, and conceive their task to be principally that of organizing the subject matter in ways by which they can most readily expound it and their pupils most easily assimilate it, they are adopting an instructional pattern. Its characteristics are formality, orderliness, and the transference of information from an authoriative source to a pupil. An educational approach makes its point of focus the learner rather than the content to be learned, and, although the teacher may be no less scholarly than his instructional counterpart, his educational priorities lie in understanding his pupils and fostering their development. Its characteristics are pupil initiative and involvement, and a care for a wide range of pupil growth. In this sense Vittorino, Erasmus, Comenius, Pestalozzi, Froebel, Makarenko, and the Progressives were the initiators of educational methods. In due course their methods were taken up by teachers in a changed context and were transformed and consolidated into new instructional patterns which tended to endure. The transition from Vittorino to Sturm, and from Pestalozzi to the Herbartians are two clear examples of the swing from educational to instructional processes. The conservatism of the teaching profession, its steady affection for routine, and the attraction of the seemingly greater efficiency of an instructional system have ensured a continuing popularity for instructional methods. The history of teaching methods might well be regarded as largely a study of various instructional patterns from which the teaching profession has had periodically to be rescued.

3.8 Teaching and Training

Teacher education is one context in which teaching occurs. It is an especially interesting context because teaching is the basis of the objectives guiding teacher education programmes as well as a process by which those objectives are attained, and the main outcome by which the success of the programmes is judged.

Efforts to define "teaching" have centered on explorations of various facets of the concept of teaching rather than on the formulation of explicit definitions. The descriptive definition of "teaching" can be stated as 'teaching is imparting knowledge or skill'. "Teaching", as success, signifies the idea that learning are in extricably intertwined. The international concept of teaching gives support to researchers who study the ways teachers think. The performance of teachers is considered as guided by their intentions, grounded in the teacher's belief system and modes of thinking. International uses of "teaching" rule out purely behaviouristic accounts of teaching. Successful teaching cannot be reduced to a set of general rules, or a prescribed pattern of behaviour, any more than the sufficient conditions of problem solving or creativity can be specified.

The normative concept of teaching requires that the activities of teaching conform to certain ethical conditions. In the normative concept, "teaching" is a generic term. It designates a family of activities : training and instructing are primary members and indoctrinating and conditioning are near relatives. Training and conditioning consist of activities that shape skills and other behaviours while instruction and indoctrination are made up of activities which knowledge and belief are induced.

Training and instruction comprise what is called teaching. Conditioning relies on neither evidence nor reasons and is deemed to be only remotely related to teaching. Training may and often does involve instruction—giving information in the form of directions, reasons, and evidence—and is thereby a form of teaching. Both instruction and indoctrination are used to induce belief just as training and conditioning are used to shape behaviour. A concept that identifies teaching with instruction and training and less so with conditioning and indoctrination, places a heavy burden upon the teacher, both pedagogically and ethically.

Training is used in a pejorative way less frequently than either "conditioning" or "indoctrination" and accordingly, has a more substantial area of overlap with "educative teaching". In many contexts, "teaching" can be substituted for "training" without a change in meaning. The focus of training is on the development of skills, on knowing - how rather than knowing - that. Teaching someone a skill requires developing the learner's capacity to respond to the unexpected, to understand what he or she is doing and why, to be intelligent and reflective in the exercise of his or her skill.

It is useful to think of teaching as involving the simultaneous performance of three tasks : (a) maintaining the classroom learning environment; (b) providing learning experiences appropriate to the changing needs of individual pupils; and (c) implementing those experiences in which the teacher is an active participant.

For convenience, performance of the first task is referred to as "environmental maintenance," the second as "managing learning," and the third as "instructing." The effects of all of the knowledge and skill a teacher possesses depend almost entirely on their being deployed appropriately, on their being used at the right time and with the right pupil; in short, on the interactive decisions the teacher makes.

Effective teaching involves a two-stage decision process. In the pre-active phase of teaching the teacher must draw on his or her own knowledge base, knowledge of pedagogy and of subject matter, of the pupils and community, of the resources available, to decide upon a plan, strategy, or model of teaching to be followed during the interactive phase of teaching. Out of this must come a set of rules that will guide the teacher's interactive decisions. In the classroom the teacher must decide what to do next according to the strategy or model he or she has decided to follow, not by any direct appeal to the knowledge base. Because the knowledge base is used in choosing the strategy or model rather than in implementing it, the choice can be rational. Because it is made outside the classroom there is time to reflect, to consult the literature, or even a colleague.

Having an adequate knowledge base means being able to do the following :

1. Plan lessons that enable students to relate new learning to prior understanding and experience.
2. Develop rapport and personal interactions with students.
3. Establish and maintain rules and routines that are fair and appropriate to students.
4. Arrange the physical and social conditions of the classroom in ways that are conducive to learning and that fit the academic task.
5. Represent and present subject matter in ways that enable students to relate new learning to prior understanding and that help students develop metacognitive strategies.
6. Assess student learning using a variety of measurement tools and adapt instruction according to the results.
7. Reflect on their own actions and students' responses in order to improve their teaching.

The idea of framing a knowledge base around tasks of teaching has a certain face validity. Teaching is a practical art and the tasks of teaching cover familiar territory. Additional support for this approach comes from research on teachers' classroom knowledge, which also uses the construct of 'tasks' to describe the way individual teachers acquire and organise their knowledge of classroom events. According to the researchers, teachers organise their knowledge around particular tasks of teaching such as teaching lessons or maintaining order. While these tasks are common to all classrooms, the meaning individual teachers bring to them is a function of their unique knowledge and experience. Furthermore, as teachers act to accomplish tasks of teaching, their understanding of what a given task involves and what it means to accomplish it changes. From this perspective, teachers learn to teach as they make sense of and take on the tasks of teaching.

3.9 Rethinking Teacher Education Programmes

Over the past decade, many schools of education have made great strides in incorporating new understandings of teaching and learning in their curriculum for prospective teachers. More attention to learning theory, cognition, and learning strategies has accompanied a deepening appreciation for content pedagogy and constructivist teaching strategies. In addition, teacher preparation and teacher induction programmes are increasingly introducing strategies that help teachers develop a reflective and problem solving orientation. This is done by engaging prospective teachers and interns in teacher research, in school-based inquiry, and in learning about students' experiences so that they are building an empirical understanding of learners and a capacity to analyze and reflect on their practice.

These efforts to develop teachers as managers of their own inquiry stands in contrast to earlier assumptions about teacher induction and about teaching generally—that beginning teachers needed to focus only on the most rudimentary tasks of teaching with basic precepts and cookbook rules to guide them and that teachers in general should be the recipients of knowledge rather than the generators of knowledge and understandings about students. The function of teacher preparation is increasingly seen as empowering teachers to own, use, and develop knowledge about teaching and learning as sophisticated and powerful as the demands of their work require.

In addition to preparation that is rigorous and relevant to today's educational needs, teacher education programmes are increasingly seeking to offer prospective teachers opportunities to work with effective guidance in diverse settings and underserved areas.

An important part of the current redesign of teacher preparation includes efforts to extend the concept of mentoring in more systematic ways within restructured school settings, especially in urban areas. A growing number of education schools are working with school systems to create institutions like professional development schools and internship sites that will allow new teachers to be inducted into schools as they must become, not only schools as they are. Too often there is a disjunction between the conceptions of good practice beginning teachers learn in their preparation programmes and those they encounter when they begin teaching. Typically, beginning teachers are placed in the most difficult schools, those with the highest rates of teacher turnover, the greatest numbers of inexperienced staff, and the least capacity to support teacher growth and development. These are also often schools where the kinds of learner-centered practices that current reforms are seeking to develop are either not well developed or not well supported. Thus, it is difficult for beginning teachers to develop ways of really connecting what they know to what students know when there are so few supports in the school environment for learning to practice in this more challenging way.

The conditions for thoughtful, adaptive teaching must be well supported by expert, experienced staff in order to be emulated by and instilled in beginning teachers. Because the development of learner-centered practice is enormously difficult, untutored novices often fail at their early attempts. The application of knowledge about learning, teaching, curriculum-building, development, motivation, and behaviour to the individual needs of diverse students is a daunting task requiring skillful observation, diagnosis, and integration of many different concepts and abilities. Unless this occurs with the support of an able mentor, the effort can quickly become overwhelming. This is one of the reasons that knowledge acquired in pre-service courses is often not put to use and that beginning teachers' practices often become less sensitive to students' needs rather than more so over the course of their initial year in teaching.

Beginning teachers must develop the ability to apply knowledge appropriately in different contexts while handling the dozens of cognitive, psychological, moral, and interpersonal demands that simultaneously require attention in a classroom. Learning to manage the different personalities and needs of twenty-five or thirty children while prioritizing and juggling often conflicting goals does not happen quickly, automatically, or easily. These are skills that have to be developed. Clinical experiences must enable teachers to learn firsthand about the variability in students' cognitive development and approaches to learning while they are supported with guided instruction and opportunities for reflection on their teaching and its effects on learners. These educative complements to classroom work should assist novices in acquiring wider repertoires of teaching strategies and help them relate problems of teaching practice to research on teaching and human development. Having these kinds of opportunities available should encourage beginners to teach reflectively, to evaluate what they are doing, to assess whether it is working and why, to understand how to make better decisions, and to juggle the many concerns of teaching.

A growing number of teacher educators have argued that professional development schools may be the best hope for addressing beginning teachers' needs. Like teaching hospitals in the medical profession, they may be structured to provide an environment in which new teachers are gradually introduced to the responsibilities of teaching and are given assistance from experienced colleagues as well as their university based teachers. In such environments, beginning teachers receive on-going evaluation and feedback from other teachers about their teaching as well as more formal learning opportunities that enable them to link theory and practice. During a formalized internship or induction year, beginning teachers have opportunities for professional development that encourage collaboration and provide the support that is associated with stronger beginning teacher commitment and efficacy.

3.10 The Prospective Model

Approaches to the development of professional skills and competencies in pre-service teachers revolve round the provision of guided experiences in school or school like situations. Almost universally, this involves the placement of student teachers in actual schools and classrooms for varying periods of time and at varying stages for their training.

Teachers training is a joint responsibility of schools and colleges of education. The total responsibility for the preparation of teachers must be shared by those who are the consumers as well as the producers. Both the schools and the colleges must work together in planning and implementation of the entire Teacher Training Programme. Structured procedure for this joint venture is highly desirable. It is, therefore felt that the Government should take necessary steps to ensure whole hearted co-operation from schools in teacher preparation programme.

Planning is the principal ingredient in the formula for success in the teacher training, which has to be done by all the three participants— the co-operating teacher, the trainee and the college supervisor. Next comes comprehensive supervision and guidance by competent and experienced persons already in the profession because it is only through careful constructive and comprehensive guidance that student teacher reaches the expected standard of the competency required for the responsible job. Such supervision must be forthcoming from the college, from the administrative officials in the schools, and most frequently of all, from the co-operating teachers. This requires mutual understanding and positive interaction among all the parties.

The term SEP emphasises that besides classroom teaching, prospective teachers under training need to know, exercise and learn how to play their other roles outside the classroom and within the school in order to give them a functional competency and perspective in their roles for shouldering the responsibilities required for the job. SEP has two very significant parts : planning of student teaching and planning of school activities in which the teacher has to play an important role.

For proper implementation of Internship in Teaching, Practice Teaching and SEP the following points are worth consideration :

- Pre-service teacher-training is to be school based. Prospective teachers are to be given on-site exposure to the realities of teaching in the schools including those in the slum areas and remote villages.
- School-based teacher education is to be made practicum based. The curriculum should involve a structured programme where the teacher -trainee has to learn to be an effective teacher by actually being involved with pupils and the community. Theory and practice are to be integrated at the earliest stage of the intern's experiences. He is to be encouraged to become a successful teacher through simple, appropriate classroom and community apprenticeship activities.
- Prospective teachers in teacher-training colleges are required to carry out some of their field works also during Internship Programme. In addition in Four Year Integrated Teacher Training Programme as in Regional Colleges/Institutes of Education (NCERT) trainees should be provided additional practical experience by doing their practicum twice : firstly in the second or third year (for some weeks) and secondly in the fourth year (for some weeks). After the first practicum, the Interns, co-operating teachers and supervisors from the Colleges of Education should discuss and endeavour to solve the problems that might arise during Interns' initial exposure to classroom teaching.
- Plunging teachers into the classroom without proper orientation has been found to be generally counter-productive and sometimes quite traumatic for Interns (Cruz, 1988). Efforts, therefore, are to be made to provide a more systematic teacher induction process. The Co-operating School may be requested to take care of the required induction of teacher trainees. Intensive seminars can be organised for prospective teachers. However, the trainees can get much help from their fellow teachers and supervisors if weekly staff meetings are organised for interaction between the two.

- Teacher educators who go out to supervise pre-service teachers during their teaching practice can also provide in-service education to school teachers.
- The Cluster Approach to teacher training can also be tried in which personnel and physical facilities between Colleges of Education can be shared by grouping teacher education institutions into clusters for the purpose of sharing resources. In India IASEs and CTEs can establish such linkages.
- Variety of field experiences should be provided to prospective teachers. There should be observational and tutorial field experiences prior to student teaching. During the initial phase one or two days per week observing or tutoring in schools and field experiences in method courses are desirable. There should be classroom observations before entering an intensive student teaching experience.
- Student-teachers may engage students in atleast two different placements so that they can experience varied classrooms.
- Recognition and financial benefit be provided to the co-operating teachers for their suprvisory works and guidance to student teachers.
- Connections among subject matter content, educational theory and practical application be strengthened (Goodlad, 1990; Schwartz, 1988; Zeichner, 1986).
- Co-operating teacher should be selected not on the basis of administrative convenience but from the point of view of educational vlaue. Sufficient training is required for co-operating teachers for their roles and sufficient contact be established for the preparation programme (Darling-Hammond and Goodwin 1993).
- Adding one year in the existing B.Ed. training programme *i.e.* enhancing B.Ed. course to two years will provide greater flexibility for the intergration of theory and practice because the extended time allows greater opportunity for an in-depth supervised internship. Adding one year in teacher preparation programme and the credit hours in professional education will

increase the amount of field-based experience (Feiman-Nemser, 1990). On the contrary a reduced professional education course reduces course work in learning and child development, and focuses on generic rather than subject – specific approaches to pedagogy (Murray, 1996).

3.10.1 Pre-Intership Orientation/Readiness Activities

Before the trainees are placed in the Co-operating Schools for Practice Teaching and Internship Activities, a Pre-Internship Orientation Programme should be organised atleast for six weeks. The planning and organisation of the programme should be done in a democratic way, seeking the help of school teacher, student-teachers and teacher-educators.

The following activities may be taken up under the orientation programme :

- Orientation of college supervisors, co-operating teachers and principals for their supervisory roles and other responsibilities for proper implementation of Internship Programme.
- Providing specific training to supervisors in techniques of teaching, and feedback.
- Training and orientation programmes for co-operating teachers (like referesher courses) in content enrichment, communication skills, and innovations in evaluation etc.
- Organisation of Co-operating School Principals' Conference for exchange of views and effective organisation of internship programme. It may include discussion on practical problems of interns, role of co-operating teachers in supervision and evaluation of interns' performance, school discipline, syllabus to be taught by interns, teaching aids, reference materials, library and laboratory to be used by interns, expectations from interns, rules and regulations of the schools, participation in school activities, physical facilities and guidance to be provided to interns, time table, community participation, new teaching methods, duration of internship, number of lessons

to be taught, and role of supervisors and co-operating school teachers during Internship.

- Orientation of educators/supervisors and co-operating teachers on how to observe lessons, how to rate, how to write comments; training on how to evaluate assignments and reports etc.
- Orientation on all the components of each assignment and writing of the report.
- Provisoin of handouts or manual for the total programme, tools, evaluation/assessment tools and other details to supervisors, co-operating teachers and Principals.
- Orientation of Interns for their field assignments and projects.
- Visits to schools to study the school environment and pupils, to observe teachers at work and various activities of the schools, observation of co-operating teachers' lessons.
- Discussion on the observed lessons of school teachers.
- Training of interns in observation schedule to develop observation skills indicating what, how, when and why to observe and also to write a concise report on observation of lessons during practice-teaching.
- Training in core-teaching skills such as
  - Skill of Class Management,
  - Skill of Set Induction,
  - Skills of Communication (*i.e.* Narration, Recitation, Dramatisation, Explanation, Demonstration, Stimulus Variation, Illustrating with Example etc.)
  - Skills of use of Teaching Aids *i.e.* selection of teaching aids; preparation of charts, models, maps, diagrams etc., operation of E.T. instruments; practice in blackboard writing including drawing, sketching, preparing tables and graphs etc.
  - Skill of Closure or Recapitulation.
  - Integration of Skills of Macrolesson.
- Use of video tape in Micro-teaching sessions. Adequate practice in simulated teaching.

- Inculcating adequate teaching competencies in the use of Audio-visual Aids and Educational Technology.
- Training in content analysis, and question paper analysis.
- Delivering lessons in simulated conditions on atleast 10 core-teaching skill lessons (5 in each teaching subject) by each teacher-trainee.
- Organisation of Demonstration lessons and holding discussions on them.
- Demonstration of atleast on one Model of Teaching.
- Practice in models of teaching.
- Training in organising school activities Co-curricular Activities and discussion sessions.
- Training and Practice in Lesson-Planning, Unit-Planning, Lesson Notes (practice in at least 2 Units, and at least 2 Lesson Plans in each subject). Preparation of Achievement Tests and Diagnostic Tests (atleast one test in both the teaching subjects).
- Orientation on the use of facilities available in schools.
- Orientation on various methods of teaching.
- Training in Role-Play, Brain-storiming and Dramatisation.
- Orientation on
  - Textbook Analysis.
  - Remedial Teaching.
  - Formulation of objectives.
  - Orientation for organising Parent Teacher Association, and MTA.
  - Orientation to Case study, Lab study, School Plant study, Study of school records, Admission procedure, Registers, Preparation of result, Fee collection etc.
  - Orientation for Class-work and Home-work.
  - Preparation of Time-Table, School—Calendar and Cumulative Records.

3.10.2 Internship Activities

The Internship Activities should include :

- Pre-placement orientation of interns atleast for one week.
- Placement of interns in the co-operating schools for atleast ten weeks keeping in view the sufficient facilities and classes available in various subjects to be taught by Interns. Organisation of meetings of interns, co-operating teachers/ principals in the respective schools.
- Job and time-table distribution
- Fixing a realistic student and supervisor ratio for effective supervisoin.
- Collaborative supervision by the method masters and the co-operating teachers with content background.
- Practice Teaching (atleast 25 Lessons in each subject).
- Use of Interaction Analysis.
- Regular supervision, evaluation and discussion.
- Participation in group discussion by the Interns, Co-operating Teachers and Supervisors.
- Atleast 25 per cent lessons must be supervised by the subject teachers/supervisors, and college supervisor, on daily lessons.
- Adopting practice of rotatory supervision.
- Use of objective tools like rating scales and checklists in the supervision.
- Preparation of lesson plans and conducting classes on practical skill based lessons.
- Practice in atleast one Models of Teaching *i.e.*, Advance Organiser, Inquiry Training, and Concept Attainment Models etc.
- Replacement of lesson plans by lesson notes as the number of lessons delivered increases. The lesson notes may include

objectives, learning material, and instructional strategy. Replacement of fixed pattern of Lesson Planning by format of Models of Teaching.

- Practice on creative teaching, child centred activities and participatory methods of teaching.
- Preparation of lesson plans and teaching by using different methods of teaching, *e.g.* project, heuristic, demonstration method etc.
- Designing the unit tests, administering them, evaluating and providing feedback to students by Interns.
- Adequate practice to Interns on learner-centred approach. Preparation of progress-reports or progress-cards.
- Use of tape record for self feedback
- Preparation of various types of Tests, Items, Scoring Key, and Marking Scheme.
- Interaction with parent (of students) during Teacher-Parent Meet.
- Training in the usage of Interview Schedules and their analysis.
- Organising subject quiz.
- Organising subject exhibitions.
- Praticipation in subject-clubs and promoting other school activities.
- Observation/Supervision of peers on practice lessons on the observation schedule (atleast 20 lessons, 10 in each subject).
- Semi-structured supervision followed by group supervision.
- Completion of field-assignment by the Interns under the guidance and supervision of the supervisors/co-operating teachers.
- Guidance by supervisors in class-management, preparation and use of teaching-learning aids.
- Conducting class tests on teaching subject.
- Sociometric study of the class.

- Organisation of co-curricular activities such as games. educational tours, cultural programmes exhibition, discussion on current topics etc., in the school under the supervision of school teachers and supervisors.
- Participation in working with community programme.
- Experience in library, laboratory and record maintenance.
- Making case studies and preparation of report of atleast two case studies of problem children/gifted children/retarded children.
- Completion of action research related to a specific school problem.
- Analysis of textbooks and question papers.
- Lab. study and school plant study.
- Preparation of school calendar.
- Study and preparation of school registers and other documents such as fee book, admission forms and admission register, attendance registers, transfer certificate, stock register etc.
- Assessment of the use of library by the students.
- Study of the school environment and its socio-cultural fabric.
- Periodical review of the progress of each intern for the entire SEP.
- Visit to various places of educational significance, such as :
  - Rural-craft centres, farms, cottage industries etc.
  - Juvenile courts, remand homes etc.
  - Special schools for the handicapped.
  - Visit to historical places, monuments, museums, industrial units and geographical places etc.
- Organisation of get together of the Co-operating School Teachers, Principal and Supervisiors on the last day of the Internship in the respective school.

3.10.3 Post-Internship Activities

- Post-Internship Seminars and Discussions on the Interns' performance.
- Evaluation of Assignments with the help of rating scales evoled on the basis of the evaluation criteria.
- Viva-voice on the Internship Experiences.
- Exhibition of Teaching Aids prepared by Interns.
- Inviting feedback from the Principals and Teachers of Co-operating Schools.
- Organising seminars of the supervisory staff to debate on issues related to supervision.
- Preparation of brief report by each Intern about his/her experience during Internship alongwith the comments and suggestions for improvement.
- Submission of the report of peer-group observation.
- Suggestions by Interns, School-teachers and Supervisors for strengthening Internship Programme.
- Best Lesson, Demonstration Week be organised. Video recordings of such lessons be done.
- Issue of letter of thanks to the co-operating schools.
- Involvement of Co-operating schools in the activities of the training colleges/institutes at other occasions also.

3.10.4 Duration of Internship Programme (Two year B.Ed. and Four year Integrated Course).

1. Pre-Internship – (First Year/Third Year)
    - Training in simulated situation in the College of Education/Teacher Training Institution for atleast six weeks. (in the First Year in the Two Year Course and in the Third Year in the Four Year Course).

- School Attachment for Two Weeks (in the first and third year respectively).

2. Internship/Practice Teaching (Second Year/Fourth Year)
   - Pre-placement orientation – One Week
   - School Attachment – (a) Ten Weeks (in the Two years Course);
     – (b) Atleast for Eight Weeks in the Four Year Integrated Course.

3.11 Induction Programme

Two major types of induction programmes are Internships and Beginning Teacher Programmes (Zeichner, 1979). Internship includes atleast half time teaching of no less than five or six months with full responsibility assigned to the interns for the groups of classes which they teach (McDonald, 1982).

- Informal support, conversations with other teachers and friends, concern for immediate and specific problems to do with school setting, the classroom, their teaching needs, more release and planning time or more time for observing other teachers, more opportunities to receive curriculum information of a specific kind on school routine, more in-classroom assistance from experienced teachers of a non-evaluative kind are of benefit in the induction programme (Grant and Zeichner, 1981).
- Induction procedure for beginning teachers should include adoption of receiving written materials on school matter; accepting advice in classroom management or help in producing programmes of work; accepting evaluation of own teaching; participation in organised consultation with experienced school personnel; attending group meetings for beginning teachers at school; observing other teachers' methods of teaching; visiting other schools for observation/consultation; conferring

informally with beginning teachers from other school; and looking at local educational resources (Tisher, 1978, 1980).

- Good induction programme should include (a) additional release time for the beginning teacher; (b) school-based support from a colleague acting as a mentor or professional tutor who also receives some additional release time plus initial and continuing training; (c) planned and systematic school-based activities including classroom observation and support; (d) planned and systmatic externally based activities organised by education authorities and college personnel; and (e) the explicit and active support of school principals and administrators. (Zeichner, 1979).
- The broad aim of the induction programme should be to offer practical and individualised help to probationers and that the main focus should be upon the problems and opportunities facing them in their own classrooms and schools (Bolam, 1973).
- Induction programmes should provide information, advice, and in-service experience to achieve following aims related to enabling teachers to make independent, professional judgements: (a) the promotion of growth and development, not simply survival skills, for all beginning teachers; (b) subject teaching skills; (c) general teaching and classroom skills; (d) colleague relationships; (e) school procedures; (f) educational administrative procedures; and (g) the teacher's personal situation.

3.12 Supervision

- Those co-operating teachers who have positive attitudes towards children, enlightened educational ideas and a commitment to teaching should be associated with teacher education programmes (Price, 1961; Finalayson and Cohen, 1967; Johnson, 1968; Yee, 1969; Peters, 1971).
- Exposure to a variety of teaching models during practice teaching periods are beneficial to the students' (prospective teachers') professional growth (Nias, 1977).

- Sufficient opportunities should be provided for private conferences, group conferences, teaching demonstrations, special duties, methods classes and tape recording of lessons (Nicklas, 1960).
- The co-operating teachers should give student teachers adequate information on the abilities, attitudes, and skills of the pupils at the beginning of the practicum so that the students will have realistic expectations of pupil performance and potential (Trimmer 1961; Johnson and Knaup, 1970).
- In case of any tension or misunderstanding between a student-teacher and co operating teacher the university/teacher education college supervisor's task is to diffuse interpersonal tensions between the co-operating teacher and student teacher, clearing the way for the student teacher's growth (Mayer and Goldsberry 1993).
- There should be an intensive supervision by tertiary staff/ university supervisor for better performance by student teachers (Stapleton, 1965). Student-teachers whose supervisors always schedule their observations well advance show a marked increase in their self concept also (Burgy, 1973).
- For the development of creative abilities supervision be done in terms of general objectives, planning and organisation. The supervisor should be aware of a greater number of factors in the student teacher's performance and be more sensitive to factors involving pupil-teacher relationships (Cicirrelli, 1969).
- There should not be conflict between the teaching ideals of the supervisor and co-operating teacher. High anxiety level and confusion are promoted where such a conflict exist with student-teachers torn between conflicting advice and criticism from the two (Sinclair and Nicoll, 1981).
- A deliberate attempt should be made to place student-teachers in teaching situations which are appropriate to their stage of professional development. High levels of stress among student teachers during the practicum in terms of lowered self-image are found when students are moved into more difficult and unfamiliar teaching situations (Coulter, 1974).

- Clear and consistent expectations, positive feedback, careful evaluation, and professional relationship which includes a generous amount of trust, support. understanding and consideration are expected from cooperating teachers (Lowther, 1968). Again student-teachers desire a co-operating teacher who offers constructive criticism, who shares ideas and materials with them, and provides such opportunities and support that they can experiment, innovate, and develop teaching strategies on their own initiative (Love and Swain, 1980).
- Supervision should be fundamentally an exercise in human relationships. The technical expertise in strategies of supervision is to be combined with sensitivity to individual students and their unique learning requirements (Lomax, 1973).
- There is a need for more organised approaches to supervision which focus on the rigorous analysis of classroom teaching in a co-operative manner. One such organised approach called clinical supervision based on first hand observation of actual teaching events, and face-to-face interaction in. the analysis of teaching behaviours and activities for instructional improvement is suggested (Goldhammer *et al.* 1980).
- Thus, supervisors must understand the importance of processes they are following in clinical supervision and they must possess specific capabilities including "skills which ensure clear communication and establish open and healthy interpersonal relations, skills in systematic and objective observation and analysis of classroom behaviours, and skills in conducting supervisory conferences, providing focussed databased feedback in a non-threatening manner, and facilitating growth in student-teachers' problem-solving abilities, with greater and more systematic participation in the student-teachers' professional development (Copeland and Boyan, 1975). The six key roles that supervisors should perform are — manager, counsellor, instructor, observer, provider of feedback, and evaluator (Turney *et al.* 1982).

3.13 Mentoring

- The mentor has most to contribute at levels of direct practice and indirect practice, whereas HEI (Higher Education Institution) tutor has a great contribution to make at levels of practical principles and disciplinary theory (Furlong, Hirst, Pocklington, and Miles, 1988). The class teachers focus largely on craft knowledge....... co-tutors concentrate on areas such as teaching dimensions, curriculum knowledge and subject matter knowledge, whereas supervisors, in seeking principle oriented outcomes, relate more to children's learning and theories and research on teaching processes (Bennett and Dunne, 1996).
- There are three models of mentoring : the apprenticeship model, the competency model, and the reflective model. Each mentor model is partial and inadequate, perhaps only appropriate at a particular stage of trainees' development (Maynard and Furlong, 1993).
- To prioritize the skills and qualities which are regarded as most important to the role as mentor the highest priority is given to interpersonal skills, over the importance given to professional experience, personal qualities, and subject specific expertise (Brooks, 1996).
- The mentor has to help prepare prospective teachers. There should be trust and respect between mentors and student teachers on personal and professional levels. The mentors should act as instructors and critics, instilling confidence as mentors go through inevitable disillusionment and doubt (Martin, 1994). Mentoring has nurturing and supportive role empowering student-teachers to engage in learning to teach as a critically reflective process (Daloz, 1986).
- The mentor as facilitator has to emphasise discussion with mentees rather than shared and team teaching. The progressively collaborative mentor has to emphasise working along side mentees, offering advice as the confidence and skills of the mentees increase. The professional friend mentor has to emphasise the importance of the mentees' actual performance

in the classroom. The classical mentor has to emphasise counselling techniques, listening to problems, and giving feedback (Saunders *et al.*, 1995).

- If teacher training aims to develop autonomous reflective teachers, mentors must engage with the individual student teacher and recognise his or her individual strengths and difficulties, not always readily expressed verbally, but perhaps manifest through the dynamics and operation of their relationship (Ronnestad and Skovholt, 1993).

3.14 Frameworks for Teacher Education Pedagogy

- The following major orientations to teacher education have substantial implications for designing and/or selection of teacher education pedagogies.

  (i) The practical/craft orientation fosters an interest in demonstration lessons, exemplary models, and apprenticeships with specially competent and committed practitioners. Here emphasis is on preparing teachers to deal effectively with the "real world" of schooling the management of classes, the conduct of lessons, and the performance of many other tasks a teacher faces throughout the school years. Cognitive psychologists extolled the virtue of situated cognition, communities of practice and apprenticeship modes of learning (Brown, Collins, and Duguid, 1989).

  (ii) The technological perspective is associated with procedures of task analysis and instructional design exemplified in programmed instruction. The most renowned version of this approach is the Performance or Competency Based Teacher Education (Gage and Winne, 1975). This orientation includes laboratory skill training methods (*e.g.* micro teaching and mini courses), intensive observation and feedback strategies, peer coaching, and training oriented simulations (Cruickshank, and Metcalf, 1990).

campus class discussions about observations as well as individual conferences with the teacher educators are recommended (Rovegno, 1992). Placements that offer multiple opportunities for student teachers to talk with their co-operating teachers are suggested (Killian and McIntyre, 1988). Weekly seminars that provide opportunities for student teachers, co-operating teachers, and university faculty to reflect about experiences through conversations are advocated (Applegate and Lasely, 1982; Zeichener and Liston, 1987).

The seminars expose misconceptions, fears and frustrations from all participants and offer opportunities to celebrate successes (Mackinnon and Grunau, 1991). It provides plurality of vision essential to comprehensive understanding of classroom processes (Elbaz, 1988).

- Supervision would provide an ideal setting for conversations about teaching (Glickman and Bey, 1990). It involves the elicitation of "Practical arguments" (Fenstermacher and Richardson, 1993).

3.14.10 Case and Case Methods

In the past few years there has been a massive increase in enthusiasm for cases and case methods in the education of teachers (Merseth, 1991 ; Sykes and Bird, 1992). Casebooks, and case methods range from short episodes to lengthy descriptions of year long experiences, from general teaching dilemmas to subject specific reasoning (Hinely and Ford, 1994; Silverman, Welty, and Lyon, 1991).

The goal of using cases as precedents is two-fold; (1) to help student teachers acquire the situated knowledge of teaching in order to "think like a teacher" (Kleinfeld, 1992), and (2) to engender habits of analysis inquiry and reflection to grow in their professional understandings and abilities. It also develops cognitive flexibility and the acquisition of knowledge (Spiro and others, 1987).

3.14.11 Cognitive Apprenticeship

The concept of apprenticeship adapts the features of traditional aprenticeship to the teaching and learning of cognitive skills in schools (Collins, Brown, and Holum, 1991). The development of critical analytic expertise and skills of deliberate action will require a learning approach that can uncover the thinking of expert teachers and make it visible to the learning practitioner.

- Reciprocal teaching, small problem solving groups, class demonstrations, control strategies to direct student learning task, and post-mortem analyses are several instructional strategies that are effective in uncovering thinking processes Clustering of student teachers within the professional practice school provides the opportunity for observation and interaction with other learners.
- Paring student teachers in one classroom or with teams of teachers encourages reciprocal teaching, one strategy in cognitive apprenticeship (Lemlech and Foliart, 1992).

3.15 Professional Development School (PDS)

Teacher preparation courses in a PDS should offer new veteran teachers opportunities to test theoretical constructs from preparatory classes against the daily press of work with students (Stallings, 1991). A PDS should create setting in which universities and schools share in the preparation of new teachers and where mutual renewal is a shared goal (Goodlad, 1993).

- To support reform teacher education faculty must redesign their courses to support on going experimentation in a setting that becomes inherently unstable as change takes hold.
- The following adaptations of campus-based programme can allow teacher preparation courses conducted in professional development schools to support school and professional renewal simultaneously:
  - (i) *Integrated Practica :* The Interns may test educational theory in practice in the Secondary Education Practicum courses.

(ii) *Results Orientation :* The Interns should make something happen in the life of the school and to use what they are learning to make a difference among students and teachers.

(iii) *Professional Portfolios :* Interns should assemble evidence that they can contribute to student learning and school change (Dollase, 1996). Interns must demonstrate mastery of learning from the teacher preparation curriculum in a school with its own unique character and evolving sense of purpose.

- While school-based interns would be completing their teaching requirements, teams of professional teachers in a PDS should be involved in a school development course, conducting research over a full school year in support of school improvement.
- The simultaneous activity of pre-service interns pursuing practicum assignments for their courses and professional teachers working together on problem-solving teams can create an enriched development setting that fosters adaptive growth.
- The co-operating school teachers should assume increasing importance in preparing the new teachers, conducting seminars, supervising interns and eventually teaching courses in the established curriculum.
- The functions of PDS are three-fold :

  (i) to serve as field placement site for teacher candidates,

  (ii) to promote the professional development of experienced teachers, and

  (iii) to advance knowledge base teaching and learning by supporting reflection, inquiry, and research.

3.16 Evaluation in Internship

There should be consistent and continuous evaluation of the progress in understanding and developing competency in teaching. Evaluation cannot take place without criticism. The student-teacher must be willing to accept suggestions and criticism. The competent supervising teacher or supervisor should offer criticism constructively with suggestions for improvement and with full understanding of the ego-involvement of the student-teacher. Again, there should be mutual acceptance of evaluative suggestions.

Evaluation in student-teaching involves much more than the awarding of grades to the student-teacher and is successful only in so far as the student-teacher himself accepts and endorses the evaluative results. While evaluating student-teacher's activities the following points should be kept in mind :

- Evaluation should be comprehensive. Even minor points must be observed and suggestions for their improvement must be provided. The various tasks and assignments should also be evaluated along with teaching. Weightage to each component of internship such as lesson plan, delivery of lesson, use of teaching aids, interaction with students, performance assessment of students, and feedback provided by the Intern should be pre-decided and used in evaluation.
- Proper guidelines be developed for the evaluation of assignments.
- Evaluation should be done by a team of evaluators.
- Field Assignments may be evaluated on the spot.
- Peer evaluation also be included in the final grading.
- Well defined and reliable rating scales be used for evaluation.
- Evaluation should be formative as well as summative. Supervisors should discuss various points of regular lessons and criticism lessons with Interns also. Formative evaluation may be done through regular discussion whereas summative through assessment of project reports.
- Evaluation should be done against the attainment of the objectives of the field experiences and assignments also.
- Evaluation may be broken down into various competencies to be developed and evaluation may be done against each competency.

- Effective tools be developed and used for the assessment of core-training, practice teaching, criticism lesson, final lesson and field assignments etc.
- The criticism lessons be supervised by a panel of supervisors, cooperating teachers for the full period comprehensively and the performance be discussed with the Interns.
- 5 per cent marks may be assigned to self-evaluation.
- Marks should be distributed to all the activities of Pre-Internship, Practice-Teaching (Regular Lessons), Criticism Lessons (in both the teaching subjects), Final Lessons (in both the teaching subjects), Assignments in subject I and II along with Education, Assessment by Co-operating School, Principal and Teachers, Peer Evaluation and self-evaluation as shown in the following table :

DISTRIBUTION OF MARKS

1.	Core-training	20%
2.	Regular lessons	20%
3.	Criticism lesson	10 %
4.	Final lesson	20%
5.	Assignment Subject I	5%
6.	Assignment Subject II	5%
7.	Educational Assignment	5%
8.	Intern's evaluation by Principal/Teachers of Co-operating Schools	5%
9.	Peer Evaluations	5%
10.	Self-Evaluation	5%

- The final grades should be awarded on the completion of Internship *i.e.*, the final result sheet should indicate the marks in theory and practice along with the grade the prospective teacher has been awarded after the completion of his teaching in a school under the supervision of a mentor. Grade should be awarded in consultation with the mentor and co-operating school principal or headmaster. Grading may be as follows :

Excellent	–	A
Good	–	B
Average	–	C
Weak	–	D
Not satisfactory	–	E

- Average of all the evaluators should be taken for finalization of result and grading.

BIBLIOGRAPHY

Abell, S.K., Dillon, D. R., Hopkins, C. J., McInerney, W. D., & O'Brien, D.G. (1995). Somebody to Count on: Mentor/Intern Relationships in a Beginning Teacher Internship Program. *Teaching and Teacher Education,* 11(2), 173-188.

Agrawal, Rekha. (1994). Teachers Effectiveness of Secondary School Teachers in Relation to Participation in Their Own Children's Academic Activities. *Jr. Ind.Ed.* Vol. 20, No.2.

Allen, D., and Ryan, K.(1969). *Microteaching. Reading.* Mass.: Addison-Wesley.

Allen, D, Ryan, K. (1969). *Microteaching.* Addison-Wesley, Reading, Massachusetts.

Allen, D. W. (1994). *An Update on Microteaching Formats.* AACTE, Chicago.

American Association of Colleges for Teacher Education (1987). Teaching Teachers: Facts and Figures I (RATE). Washington, D. C.

Applegate, J.H., and Lasley, T.J. (1982). "Cooperating Teachers' Problems with Preservice Field Experience Students." *Journal of Teacher Education,* 33(2), 15-18.

Atkinson, R. C., & Shiffrin, R. M. (1971). The Control of Short Term Memory. *Scientific American*, 225, 82-90.

Atreya, J. S. (1989). A Study of Teachers' Values and Job Satisfaction in Relation to Their Teaching Effectiveness at Degree College Level. Ph.D. Edu. Agra Univ.

Bain, C. (1991, October). "Student Teaching Traids: Perceptions of Participant Roles". Paper Presented at the Annual Meeting of the Northern Rocky Mountain Educational Association, Denver.

Ball, D.L. and McDiarmid, G.W. (1990), "The Subject-Matter Preparation of Teachers". In W.R. Houston (ed.) *Hand Book of Research on Teacher Education.* Macmillan. New York.

Barrows, L. K. (1 979). "Power Relationships in the Student Teaching Triad". Paper Presented at the Annual Meeting of the American Educational Research Association, San Francisco. (ERIC Document Reproduction Service No. ED 173 335).

Barrows, L. (1979). "Power Relationships in the Student Teacher Triad". Paper Presented at the Annual Meeting of the American Educational Research Association, Washington, DC.

Basi, Satpal Kaur (1991). *A Study of Teaching Competency of Language Teachers in Relation to Their Job Satisfaction,* Locus of Control and Proffesional Burnout, Ph.D., Edu. Punjab Univ.

Baveja, B. (1989). *An Experimental Study of Information Processing Models of Teaching in Schools of India.* Ph.D. Edu. Univ. of Delhi.

Bawa, M. S. (1984). *Effectiveness of Micro Teaching with Planned Integration Training,* Following Summative Model of Micro Teaching without Planned Integration Training on the General Teaching Competence of Teacher Trainees. Ph.D. Edu. Delhi Univ.

Bellack, A.A., Kliebard, H.M., Hyman, R.T. and Smith, F.L. (1966). *The Language of the Classroom.* Teachers College Press, New York.

Bennett, N, & Carre, C. (1993). *Learning to Teach.* Routledge, London

Bennett, N., & Dunne, E. (1996, April). "Mentoring Processes in School Based Training. Paper Presented at the Annual Meeting of the American Educational Research Association, New York.

Bennie, William A. (1972). *Supervising Clinical /Experiences in the Classroom*. Harper & Row, New York.

Berliner, D. (1987). Ways of Thinking About Students and Classrooms by More and Less Experienced Teachers. In J. Calderhead (Ed.) *Exploring Teachers' Thinking* (60-84). London : Cassell.

Bestor, A. (1953). *The Restoration of Learning Knopf.* New York.

Bhagoliwal, S. (1982). *A Study of Personality Characteristics Associated with Teaching Effectiveness as Seen Through Rorschach Technique.* Ph.D. Edu., Allahabad Univ.

Bhasin, C. (1988). Teaching Aptitude and its Relationship with Teaching Effectiveness of the Higher Secondary School Teachers in Relation to the Modern Community. Ph.D. Edu. Rani Durgavati Vishwavidyalya, Jabalpur.

Bhatnagar, T.N.S. (1980). *Studies and Literature on Student Teaching and Other Practical Work in the B.Ed. Programme in India* - Review. Deptt. of Teacher Ed. Project NCERT. New Delhi.

Bhattacharjee, (1981). *Effectiveness of Micro Teaching in Developing Teaching Competence.* Extension Service Deptt. Post Graduate Training College, Shillong.

Bhatt, M.M. (1 966). *Kapasan Scheme of Improvement in Teacher Training.* SIERT Rajasthan.

Bloom, B.S. (ed.), Engethart, M.D., Furst, E.J., Hill, W.H. and Krathwohl, D.R. (1956). *Taxonomy of Educational Objectives : The Classification of Educational Goals.* Handbook I : The Cognitive Domain. Longmans Green, New York.

Blumberg, A., Amidon, E. (1965). Teacher Perceptions of Supervisor Teacher Interaction. *Administrators Notebook* 14:1-4.

Blumberg, A., Weber, W. (1968). Teacher Morale as Function of Perceived Supervisor Behavioural Style. *J. Educ. Res.* 62: 109-13.

Boden, M. (1992). *The Creative Mind : Myths and Mechanisms.* Basic Books, New York .

Bolam, R. (1973). "Induction Programmes for Probationary Teachers" : A Report on the Action Research Project Funded by the Department of Education and Science and Carried out at the University of Bristol School of Education Research Unit, 1968-72. University of Bristol School of Education, Bristol.

Bolin, F.S. (1988). "Helping Student Teachers Think About Teaching." *Journal of Teacher Education,* 39(2), 48-54.

Booth, M. (1993). The Effectiveness and Role of the Mentor in School : The Students' View. *Cambridge Journal of Education,* 23(2), 185-197.

Borg, W. R. (1972). The Minicourse as a Vehicle for Changing Teacher Behaviour : A Three Year Follow-up. *J. Educ. Psychol.* 63: 572-79.

Boyan N. J, Copeland W. D. (1978). Instructional Supervision *Training Program. Merrill,* Columbus, Ohio.

Boydell, D. (1986). Issues in Teaching Practice Supervision Research: A Review of the Literature. *Teaching and Teacher Education*, 2(2), 115-125.

Brooks, V. (1996, February). *Mentoring : The Interpersonal Dimension.* 'Teacher Development, pp. 5-10.

Brown, G. A (1975). Microteaching : Research and Developments. In :Changan G, Delamont S (eds.) *Frontiers of Classroom Research.* National Foundation for Educational Research, Slough.

Brown, J. S., Collins, A., and Duguid, P. (1989). "Situated Cognition and the Culture of Learning." *Educational Researcher,* 18 (1), 32-42.

Brown, L., and Gliessman, D.H. (1987). "The Role of Interactive Video in the Acquisition of Teaching Skills." In E.D. Doak T. Hipple, and M.Keith (eds.), *Simulation and Clinical Knowledge in Teacher Education.* College of Ed. Univ. of Tennessee. Knoxville.

Bruner, J. S. (1990). *Acts of Meaning* : Harward Univ. Press. Cambridge, M.A.

Buchmann, M. (1987). "Teaching Knowledge : The Lights That Teachers Live" by (Issue Paper No.87-1) : National Center for Research on Teacher Learning. East Lansing, Mich.

Buch, M.B. (ed.) (1974). *A Survey of Research in Education.* CASE Baroda.

Buch, M.B. (ed.) (1979). *Second Survey of Research in Education.* Soc. Edl. Res. & Dev., Baroda.

Buch, M.B. (Chief Ed.) (1986). Third Survey of Research in Education. N.C.E.R.T., New Delhi.

Buch, M.B. (Chief Ed.) (1991). Fourth Survey of Research in Education. N.C.E.R.T., New Delhi.

Buddisagar, M. (1987). Development and Comparison of Instructional Material Developed by Using Advance Organizer Model and Operant Conditioning Model for Teaching Educational Psychology to B.Ed. Students. Ph.D. Edu., DAVV Indore.

Bunting, C. (1988). Cooperating Teachers and the Changing Views of Teacher Candidates. *Journal of Teacher Education,* 39(2), 42-46.

Burgy, D.R. (1973). Developing Good Teachers by Strengthening Student Teachers' Self Concepts. *ERIC Document No.* ED087774.

Butts, D. C. (1977). An Assessment of Microteaching in the Context of the Graduate Training Year. In: McIntyre D. I., Macleaod G. R., Griffiths R (eds.).

Calderhead, J., & Robson, M. (1991). Images of Teaching : Student Teachers' Early Conceptions of Classroom Practice. *Teaching and Teacher Education*, & (1), 1-8.

Cameron-Jones, M., & O' Hara, P. (1997). Support and Challenge in Teacher Education. *British Educational Research Journal,* 23 (1), 15-23.

Carnegie Forum on Education and the Economy (1986). A Nation

Prepared: Teachers for the 21 st Century. Carnegie Foundation. New York.

Carter, K., and Doyle, W. (1987). "Teachers' Knowledge Structures and Comprehension Processes". In J. Calderhead (ed)., *Exploring Teachers' Thinking: Cassell Educational*, London.

Carter, K., and Gonzalez, L. (1993). Beginning Teachers' Knowledge of Classrooms Events." *Journal of Teacher Education*, 44, 223-232.

Carter, K., and Unkelesbay, R. (1989). "Cases in Teaching and Law." *Journal of Curriculum Studies*, 21, 527-536.

Carter, K. (1990). "Teachers' Knowledge and Learning to Teach." In W.R. Houston (ed.), *Handbook of Research on Teacher Education*. Macmillan, New York.

Carter, K. (1993) "The Place of Story in Research on Teaching and Teacher Education." *Educational Researcher*, 22 (1). 5-12.

Carter, K. (1994). Preservice Teachers' Well-Remembered Events and the Acquisition of Event-Structures Knowledge." *Journal of Curriculum Studies*, 26, 235-252.

Carr, W., and Kemmis, S. (1986). *Becoming Critical: Education, Knowledge, and Action Research*. Falmer Press. Washington D.C.

Chathley, (1984). *An Experimental Study of the Teaching Competency at Macrolevel* as a Function of Training in Micro Skills Among the Prospective Secondary School Teachers in Relation to the Integration of Skills and Subject Area. Ph.D Ed. Pan. University.

Chaudhary, K., (1989). Teaching of Concepts Through Concept Attainment Model and Facts Through Traditional Teaching: *Competency in Teaching Skills of Preservice Teachers*. Adarsh Comprehensive College of Education and Research. Pune.

Chitriv, U.G., (1983). *Evaluating Differential Effectiveness of Ausubel and Bruner Strategies for Acquisition of Concepts in Mathematics*. Ph.D. Edu. Nagpur University, Nagpur.

Cicirelli, V.G. (1969). University Supervisors' Creative Ability and Their Appraisal of Student Teachers' Performance: An Exploratory Study. *J. Educ. Res.* 62: 375-81.

Clarke, R.J., and La Londe, D.E. (1992). "A Case for Department-Based Professional Development Sites for Secondary Teacher Education." *Journal of Teacher Education*, 43 (1), 35-41.

Clarke, S.C.T. (1970). 'General Teaching Theory'. Jr. Teach. Ed. 21, 3.

Clandinin, D.J. (1992). "Narrative and Story in Teacher Education". In T. Russell and H. Munby (eds.). *Teachers and Teaching: From Classroom to Reflection.* Falmer Press, Washington, D.C.

Cogan, M.L., (1973). *Clinical Supervision.* Houghton Mifflin, Boston, Massachusetts.

Cohen, L., (1969). Students' Perceptions of the School Practice Period. *Res. Educ.* 2: 52-58.

Coker, H., Medley, D.M., Soar, R.S. (1980). How Valid are Expert Opinions About Effective Teaching? *Phi. Delta Kappan*, 62: 131-34, 149.

Cole, A.L., & Knowles, J.G. (1993). Shattered Images: Understanding Expectations and Realities of Field Experiences. *Teaching and Teacher Education*, 9 (5/6), 457-471).

Collins, R., Brown, I., and Holum, A. (1991). "Cognitive Apprenticeship: Teaching the Crafts of Reading, Writing, and Mathematics. American Educator, 15 (3), 6-11, 38-46.

Connelly, F.M., and Clandinin, D.J. (1990). Stories of Experience and Narrative Inquiry." *Educational Researcher*, 19 (5), 2-14.

Cope, E. (1971a) *School Experience in Teacher Education.* University of Bristol, Bristol.

Cope, E. (1971b) *A Study of School Supervised Practice.* University of *Bristol*, Bristol.

Copeland W.D., Boyan, N. J. (1975). Training in Instructional Supervision : Improving the Influence of the Co-operating Teacher. In: Heidelbach R. (ed.), *Developing Supervisory Practice : Selected Papers*. Association of Teacher Eductors, Washington, DC.

Copeland, W.D., Doyle W. (1973). Laboratory Skill Training and Student Teacher Classroom Performance. *J. Exp. Educ*. 52: 16-21 .

Copeland, W. D. (1975).The Relationship Between Microteaching and Student Performance. *J. Educ. Res.* 68: 289-93.

Copeland, W.D. (1977). Some Factors Related to Student Teacher Classroom Performance Following Microteaching Training. *Am. Educ. Res.* J. 14: 147-57.

Copeland W. D. (1982). "Laboratory Experiences in Teacher Education." In H. E. Mitzel (ed.), *Encyclopedia of Educational Research*, Free Press, New York.

Coulter, F. (1974). The Effects of Practice Teaching on Professional Self Image. *Aust. J. Educ*. 18: 49-59.

Coulter, F. (1975). "Perceptions of Classroom Behaviour by Supervisors and Student Teachers". Paper Presented at the National Conference on Teacher Education and the Practicum, Perth.

Crow, N. A. (1987). "Preservice Teacher's Biography: A Case Study." Paper Presented at the Annual Meeting of the American Educational Research Association Washington, D.C.

Cruickshank, D.R., and Metcalf, K.K. (1990). "Training Within Teacher Preparation." In W. R. Houston (ed.), *Handbook of Research on Teacher Education*. Macmillan. New York.

Cruz, Leonardo de la (1988). Development and Reform in Teacher Education. Bulletin of the UNESCO, PROAP. No. 29.

Das, R.C., Passi, B.K. and Singh, L.C. (1976). *A Study of the Effectiveness of Micro-Teaching in the Training of Teacher*, NCERT, New Delhi and CASE, Baroda.

Daloz, L. (1986). *Effective Teaching and Mentoring*. Jossey-Bass. San Francisco.

Darwin, C. J., Turvey, M.T., & Crowder, R. G. (1972). An Auditor Analogue of the Sperting Partial Report Procedure : Evidence for Brief Auditory Storage. *Cognitive Psychology*, 3, 255-267.

Deo, D.S. (1985). *To Study the Practical Programme Other Than Practice Teaching in Teacher Education Institutions*. Ph.D. Edu. Delhi Univ. Delhi.

Department for Education. (1992). Initial Teacher Training (Secondary Phase). Circular 9/92. Her Majesty's Stationery Office (HmSO), London.

Derrick, T. (1971). Teacher Training and School Practice. *Educational Researchers*, 13, 106-112.

Dholakia, J .V. (1980). *Effects of Observers and Feedback Upon Changing the Classroom Performance of Pupil - Teacher*, Ph.D. Edu., MS Univ. Baroda.

Dogra, N. (1986) *Effect of Training in Concept Development Strategies Upon Classroom Communication Behaviour Patterns*. Ph. D. Edu., Pan Univ. Patna.

Dollase, R. (1996). The Vermont Experiment in State-Mandated Portfolio Approval. *Journal of Teacher Education*, 47, 85-98.

Donald, R. Cruickshand and Frank W. Broadbent (1970). *Simulation in Preparing School Personnel*. ERIC Clearinghouse on Teacher Education, Washington, D.C.

Dorothy, S. Blackmore. (1968). "Integration of Theory and Practice in Internship". *Internships in Teacher Education*. Association for Student Teaching, 47th Year book, Washington, D.C.

Doyle, W. (1990). "Case Methods in the Education of Teachers," *Teacher Education Quarterly*, 17, 7-15.

Dunkin, M.J. (1976). Towards Taking Some of the fun out of the Technical Skills Approach to Teacher Effectiveness. *South Pac. J. Teach. Educ.* 4(2): 131-39.

Dwight, W. Allen. (1994). *An Update on Microteaching* Formats. Old Dominion University. Norfolk. VA 23529.

Dwight, K. Curtis, (ed.) (1957). Achieving Quality in Off Campus Professional Laboratory Experiences Bulletin No.8. Association for Student Teaching, Washington, D.C.

Dwight, K. Curtis, (1994). *An Update on Microteaching Formats.* AACTE - Chicago.

EdCIL, (1987). *Programme of Improvement of Secondary Teacher Education Institutions,* Educational Consultants India Ltd. New Delhi.

Ekbote, E.R. (1987). *Development of a Strategy for Integration of Skills in Teacher Training.* Ph.D. Edu. MS Univ. Baroda.

Elbaz, F. (1988). "Critical Reflection on Teaching: Insights from Friere." *Journal of Education for Teaching,* 1 4, 171 -181.

Elbaz, F. (1991). "Research on Teachers' Knowledge: The Evolution of a Discourse." *Journal of Curriculum Studies,* 23, l-19.

Elliott, B., & Calderhead, J. (1993). Mentoring for Teacher Development : Possibilities and Caveats. In D. McIntyre, H. Hagger, & M. Wilkin (Eds.), *Mentoring : Perspectives on School-Based Teacher Education* (pp. 166-189). Kogan Page. London.

Ellwein, M. C., Graue, M., & Comfort, R.E. (1990). Talking About Instruction: Student Teachers' Reflections on Success and Failure in the Classroom. *Journal of Teacher Education,* 41(4), 3-14.

Evertson, C.M., and Green, J. L. (1986). "Observation and Inquiry and Method." In M.C. Wittrock (ed.), *Handbook of Research on Teaching.* (3rd ed.). Macmillan. New York.

Feiman-Nemser, S. (1983). "Learning to Teach." In L.S. Shulman and G. Sykes (eds.). *Handbook of Teaching and Policy.* White Plains, Logman. N. Y.

Feiman-Nemser, S. (1990). "Teacher Preparation : Structural and Conceptual Alternatives." In W.R. Houston (ed.), Handbook of Research on Teacher Education. Macmillan. New York.

Feiman-Nemser, S., Parker, M. B., & Zeichner, K. (1993). Are Mentor Teachers Teacher Educators? In D. McIntyre, H. Hagger, & M. Wilking (Eds.), *Mentoring : Perspectives on School-Based Teacher Education* (pp.147-165). Kogan Page. London.

Felzen, E. & Anisfeld, M. (1970). Semantic and Phonetic Relations in False Recognition of Words by Third and Sixth Grade Children. *Development Psychology* 3, 163-168.

Fenstermacher, G.D., and Richardson, V. (1993). "The Elicitation and Reconstruction of Practical Arguments in Teaching." *Journal of Curriculum Studies,* 25, 101-114.

Field, B. (1994). The New Role of the Teacher : Mentoring. In B. Field & T. Field (Eds.), *Teachers as Mentors : A Practical Guide* (pp. 63-77). Falmer. London.

Finlayson, D. S., Cohen, L. (1967). The Teacher's Role. A Comparative Study of the Conceptions of College of Education Students and Head Teachers, *Br.J. Educ. Psychol.* 37: 22-31.

Fishter, B. L. (1989). Differences Between Supervision of Beginning and Advanced Therapists: Hogan's Hypothesis Empirically Revisited. *The Clinical Supervisor*, 7, 57-74.

Fitch, T. C. (1970). Role Expectations for Intern Consultants : Views of Intern Teachers and Intern Consultants in the Michigan State University Elementary Intern Program (Doctoral Dissertation, Michigan State University) Dissertation Abstracts International 1971, 31: 1115A (University Microfilms No.70-16,663).

Flanders, N. (1961). "Interaction Analysis: A Technique for Quantifying Teacher Influence". Paper Presented to the A.E.R.A. (mimeo).

Flanders, N. A. (1970). *Analyzing Teaching Behaviour. Reading,* Addison-Wesley. Mass.

Flint, S. H. (1965). The Relationship between the Classroom Verbal

Behaviour of Student Teachers and the Classroom Verbal Behaviour of Their Cooperating Teachers (Doctoral Dissertation, Teachers College, Columbia University) Dissertation Abstracts International 1966 26: 4480 (University Microfilms No.65-14,965).

Flavell, J. H., Miller, P.H., and Miller, S.A. (1993). *Cognitive Development* (2nd ed.), Prentice-Hall. Englewood Cliff, NJ.

Frankena, W. (1973). *Ethics*. Prentice-Hall. Englewood Cliffs, NJ.

Fuller, F.F. (1969). Concerns of American Teachers : A Developmental Conceptualization. *American Educational Research Journal,* 6, 207-226.

Furlong, J., Jirst, P. H., Pocklington, K., & Miles, S. (1988). *Initial Teacher Training and the School.* Open University Press. Milton Keynes, UK.

Gage, N.L., and Winne, P. H. (1975). "Performance-Based Teacher Education." In K.Ryan (ed.), *Teacher Education*. (74th Yearbook of the National Society for the Study of Education, Part 2). University of Chicago Press, Chicago.

Gallemore, S. (1981). Perceptions About the Objectives of Student Teaching. *Research Quarterly for Exercise and Sport,* 52(2), 180-190.

Gardner, H. (1983). *Frames of Mind : The Theory of Multiple Intelligences*. Basic Books. New York.

Garrison, J. W. (1988). "Democracy, Scientific Knowledge, and Teacher Empowerment." *Teachers College Record,* 89, 487-504.

Getzels, J. W. and Jackson, P. W. (1963). 'The Teachers Personality and Characteristics' . In Gage, N.L. (ed.) *Handbook of Research on Teaching*. Rand Mc Nally, Chicago.

Ghosh. S. K. (1986). *Effects of Variation in Advance Organisers on the Cognitive Subsumption in Life Science* Ph.D. Edu. Kal. U.

Govinda, R. (1976). Development of Programmed Text on Educational Evaluation and Experimentally Studying its

Effectiveness as Instructional Material for B.Ed. Students. Ph.D. Edu. M.S. Univ.

Glickman, C., & Bey, T. (1990). Supervision. In W. R. Houston (ed.), *Handbook of Research on Teacher Education* (pp.549-566). Macmillan. New York.

Glickman, C. (1990). *Supervision of Instruction : A Developmental Approach* (2nd ed.). Allyn and Bacon. Boston.

Gliessman, D.H. (1984). "Changing Teacher Performance." In L.G. Katz and J. D. Raths (eds.), *Advances in Teacher Education,* Vol. I. Ablex. Norwood, N.J.

Gliessman, D. H. (1987). "Conceptual Instruction and Intervention as Methods of Acquiring Teaching Skills." *International Journal of Educational Research,* 1 1,149-154.

Goldhammer R., Anderson R. H., Krajewsky J. J. (1980) *Clinical Supervision Special Methods for the Supervision of Teachers,* 2nd edn. Holt, Rinehart and Winston, New York.

Goodlad, J. I. (1990). *Teachers for Our Nation's Schools*. Jossey-Bass. San Francisco.

Goodlad, J. I. (1993). Why We Need a Complete Redesign of Teacher Education. *Educational Leadership,* 49(3), 4-10.

Goodwon, I. F. (ed.) (1992). Studying Teachers' Lives. Teachers College Press. New York.

Grant C. A., Zeichner K. M. (1981). Inservice Support for the First Year: The State of the Scene. *J. Res. Devel. Educ.* 14: 99-111 .

Grant, G. E. (1992). "Using Cases to Develop Teacher Knowledge: A Cautionary Tale." In J. H. Shulman (ed.), Case Methods in Teacher Education. Teachers College Press. New York.

Greenwood, G. E., and Parkay, F. W. (1989). *Case Studies for Teacher Decision Making*. Random House. New York.

Griffin, G. (1989). A Descriptive Study of Student Teaching. *The Elementary School Journal,* 89, 343-364.

Grimmett, P. P., and Mackinnon, A. M. (1992). "Craft Knowledge and the Education of Teachers." In G. E. Grant (ed.), *Review of Research in Education,* Vol. 18. American Educational Research Association. Washington, D. C.

Grimmett, P. & Ratzlaff, H. (1986). Expectations for the Cooperating Teacher Role. *Journal of Teacher Education,* 37, 41-48.

Grossman, P.L. (1990). *The Making of a Teacher : Teacher Knowledge and Teacher Education.* Teachers College Press. New York.

Gudmundsdottir, S. (1991). "Story-maker, Story-teller: Narrative Structures in Curriculum." *Journal of Curriculum Studies,* 23, 207-218.

Gupta, Arun K., Zadoo, C.K., Bhan, I., Tikku, K. Balia, J.N. (1992). The Impact of Teaching Kit on the Trainees : An Evaluative Study. *Jr. Ind. Edu.* Vol.16, No.5.

Gupta, C. (1983). *An Experimental Study of the Correlates of Teacher Performance in Simulated Teaching at Secondary Level,* Ph.D. Edu., Meerut. Univ. Meerut.

Gupta, R.P. (1979). *A Study of Some Factors Considered to be Helpful in Class Teaching.* Ph.D. Edu. Lucknow Univ. Lucknow.

Gupta, S. (1991). Effectiveness of Advance Organizer Model of Ausubel in Developing Teaching Competence of Student Teachers and Their Attitude Towards Teaching: An Experiment. Ph.D., Educ. Agra Univ.

Gupta, V.P., Sindhu, R.S., Gupta, S.K., Sharma, R., and Khan, Z.A. (1995). *Documentation of In-service Teachers Training Practices in Western Region of India.* R.I.E. (NCERT) Bhopal.

Guralnik, David B. (ed.) (1975). *Webster's New World Dictionary.* Oxford & IBH Pub. Co. New Delhi.

Guyton, E., and McIntyre, D.J. (1990). "Student Teaching and School Experiences." In W.R. Houston (ed.), *Handbook of Research on Teacher Education.* Macmillan. New York.

Haggerty, L. (1995). The Use of Content Analysis to Explore Conversations Between School Teacher Mentors and Student

Teachers. *British Educational Research Journal*, 21 (2), 183-197.

Hall, Colville; Mac Donald, Suzanne, and Smolen, Lynn. (1995). Preparing Preservice Teachers for Diversity in Learners. *Jr. Teacher Edu.* Vol.46, No.4.

Hersey, P., & Blanchard, K. (1977). *Management of Organizational Behaviour Utilizing Human Resources* (3rd ed.). Prentice-Hall. Englewood Cliffs, NJ.

Hillard, Pauline and Charles, L. Durrance (1968). Guiding Student Teaching Experiences, *Bulletin No. 1.* Rev. Association for Student Teaching. Washington, D.C.

Hinely, R., and Ford, K. (1994). *Education in Edge City: Cases for Reflection and Action.* St.Martin's Press. New York.

Holmes Group (1986). *Tomorrow's Teachers*. Homes Group. East Lansing, Mich.

Holmes Group (1986). *Tomorrow's Teachers*. East Lansing, Holmes Group. Mich .

Holt-Reynolds, D. (1992). Personal History-Based Beliefs and Relevant Prior Knowledge in Course Work. *American Educational Research Journal*, 29(2), 325-349.

Hoover, Kenneth H. (1964). *Learning and Teaching in the Secondary School.* Allyn and Bacon, Inc. Boston.

Horton, L. & Harvey, K. (1979). Preparing Cooperating Teachers : The Role of the University Supervisor. *Peabody Journal of Education,* 57(1), 56-60.

Hoy, W., & Woolfolk, A. (1989). Supervising Student Teachers. In A. Woolfok (Ed.), *Research Perspectives on the Graduate Preparation of Teachers* (pp. 108-131). Prentice Hall. Englewood Cliffs. NJ.

Howsam, R. B., Corrigan, D. C., Denmark, G. W., and Nash, R. J. (1976). *Educating a Profession.* American Association of Colleges for Teacher Education. Washington, D. C.

Jain, R. (1977). Proficiency in Teaching as a Function of Creativity, Intelligence, and Interest. Ph.D.Psy. Agra Univ. Agra.

Jangira, N.K., and Dhaudiyal, N.C. (1981). Effect of Classroom Behaviour Training (CBT) on the Classroom Questioning Behaviour of Teachers, NCERT, New Delhi.

Jangira, N.K. (1973). Classroom Behaviour Training of Teachers and its Relationship With Some Selected Measures of Pupils' Criteria of Teacher Effectiveness, Ph.D. Edu. M.S. Univ. Baroda.

Jangira, N. K., Singh, A., Mattoo, B. K. (1980). Use of Microteaching for Improving General Teaching Competence of In-Service Teachers — A Field Experiment, Deptt. of Teacher Education, NCERT, New Delhi.

John. G. Chaltas *et al.* (1968). "The Supervision of Intern Teachers," Internship in Teacher Education. Association for Student Teaching, 47th Yearbook, Washington, D.C.

Johnson J. S. (1968). Change in Student Teacher Dogmatism. *J. Educ. Res*. 62: 224-26.

Johnson, S. (1993). A Case for the Person in Curriculum Deliberation. *Teaching and Teacher Education*, 9(5/6), 473-483.

Johnson W.D, Knaupp J. E. (1970). Trainee Role Expectations for the Micro Teaching Supervisor. *J. Teach. Educ.* 21: 396-401

Joshi, D.C. (1972). *A Study of Innovations and Changes in Teachers Colleges*. Ph.D. Education. Udaipur Univ. Udaipur.

Joshi, S. M., and Kumar, S. (1983). Effect of Skill-Based Approach and Decision-Making Ability on the Development of Teaching Competence. Independent Study. M. S. Univ. Baroda.

Joyce, B., and Showers, B. (1982). "Transfer of Training: The Contribution of Coaching." *Journal of Education*, 163, 163-172.

Joyce, B. R, and Clift, R. T. (1984). "The Phoenix Agenda : Essential Reform in Teacher Education." *Educational Researcher*, 13, 5-18.

Joyce, B. R., Harrotunian, B. (1967). *The Structure of Teaching Science Research Associates*, Chicago, Illinois.

Kadushin, A. (1974). *Supervisor-Supervisee : A Survey. Social Work*, 19, 288-298.

Kadwadkar, S.D. (1984). A Critical Enquiry into Professional Courses for College Teachers in India. Ph.D. Edu. Kar. Univ.

Kagan, D. (1987). Cognitive Level of Student Teachers and Their Perceptions of Cooperating Teachers. *Alberta Journal of Educational Research*, 33, 180-190.

Kagan, D.M . (1992). Professional Growth Among Preservice and Beginning Teachers. *Review of Educational Research*, 62(2), 129-169.

Kakkad, G.M. (1983). Secondary Teacher Education Curriculum – An Analytical Study for Developing Teacher Education Programme. Ph.D. Edu. Nag. Univ. Nagpur.

Kalyanpurkar, S. (1986). The Effect of Micro-Teaching on the Teaching Competence of Inservice Teachers and its Impact on Pupils' Attainment and Pupils' Liking, Ph.D.Ed. DAVV Indore.

Kanwal, N. (1979). The Impact of Feedback on Modifying Teacher Behaviour — A Microteaching Approach, Ph.D. Edu, Pan. Univ.

Karmos, A, & Jacko, C. (1977). The Role of Significant Others During the Student Teaching Experience. *Journal of Teacher Education*, 28(5), 51-55.

Kauffman, D. (1992). Supervision of Student Teachers. Eric Digest. (ERIC Reproduction Service No. ED 344 973).

Kaul, L. (1972). Factorial Study of Certain Personality Variables of Popular Teacher in Secondary Schools, Ph.D. Edn. Kur. V.

Kaushik, N. K. (1988). The Long-Term Effect of Advance Organisers Upon Achievement in Biology in Relation to Reading Ability, Intelligence and Scientific Attitude. Ph.D. Edu. DAVV Indore.

Kestner, James L. (1994). New Teacher Induction : Findings of the Research and Implications for Minority Groups .Jr. Teacher Edu. Vol.45 No. 1 .

Killian, J.E., and McIntyre, D.J. (1988). "Grade Level as a Factor in Participation During Early Field Experiences." *Journal of Teacher Education*, 39(2), 36-41.

Kieinfeld, J. (1992). "Learning to Think Like a Teacher: The Study of Cases." In J. H. Shulman {ed.), *Case Methods in Teacher Education:* New York: Teacher College Press.

Knowles, J.G., and Holt-Reynolds, D. (1991). "Shaping Pedagogies Through Personal Histories in Preservice Teacher Education." *Teachers College Record*, 93, 87-113.

Knowles, J. G., (1992). "Models for Understanding Preservice and Beginning Teachers' Biographies: Illustrations from Case Studies." In I.F. Goodson (ed.), *Studying Teachers' Lives*. Teachers College Press. New York.

Koehler, V. (1988). Barriers to the Effective Supervision of Student Teaching A Field Study. *Journal of Teacher Education*, 39(2), 28-34.

Koerner, M. (1992). The Cooperating Teacher : An Ambivalent Participant in Student Teaching. *Journal of Teacher Education*, 43 (1), 46-56.

Kounin, J.S. (1970). *Discipline and Group Management in Classrooms*. Holt, Rinehart & Winston. New York.

Kowalski, T. J., Weaver, R. A., and Hensen, K. T. (1990). *Case Studies in Teaching*. Longman. White Plains, N.Y.

Kran. K. (1983). Phases of the Mentor Relationship. *Administrative Science Quarterly*, p.26.

Krathwohl, D.R. Bloom, B. S. and Masia, B. (1964). Taxonomy of Educational Objectives : The Classification of Educational Goals. Handbook II: The Affective Domain. David Mckay. New York.

Kremer-Hayon, L., & Wubbels, T. (1992). Interpersonal Relationship of Cooperating Teachers and Student Teachers' Satisfaction with Supervision. *Journal of Classroom Interaction*, 27(1), 31-38.

Kudesia, U.C. (1986). A Study of the Teaching Aspects as Viewed by the Polytechnic Teachers of Induction Programme. TTTI, Bhopal.

Kukreti, B. R. (1992). A Study of Some Psychological Correlates of Successful Teachers. Ph.D., Edu. Rohilkhand Univ.

Kulandaivel, K. and Rao, T.R.S., (1968). *Qualities of a Good Teacher and a Good Student* (a Study in Student Ratings), R.K. Mission Vidyalaya, Coimbatore.

Lemma, P. (1993). The Cooperating Teacher as Supervisor: A Case Study. *Journal of Curriculum and Supervision*, 8(4), 329-342.

Lemlech, J. K., and Foliart, H. (1992). "Restructuring to Become a Professional Practice School: Stages of Collegiality and the Development of Professionalism." Paper Presented at Annual Meeting of American Educational Research Association, San Francisco.

Leo-Nyquist, D. (1990, Spring-Summer). *Professional Development Schools*. Country Teacher, 10, p. 1.

Levis, D., Thompson, H., Mitchell, J. (1974). An Assessment of Alternative Techniques to Practice Teaching and an Examination of Selected Variables within a Microteaching Format.

Little, J. W. (1992). Teacher Development and Educational Policy. In M. Fullan & A. Hargreaves (Eds.), *Teacher Development and Educational Change* (pp. 57-84). Falmer, London.

Loadman, W.E. Mahon, J.M. (1973). "A Study of the Relationship Between the Rankings of Supervising Teacher Effectiveness and Attitude Toward Education". Paper Presented at the Annual Meeting of the American Educational Research Association, New Orleans.

Lomax D.E. (ed.) (1973). *The Education of Teachers in Britain*. Wiley, London.

Love, J., Swain, M. (1980). "Success in Practicum Programs: Student Teachers' Perceptions". Paper Presented at Conference on the Role of School Experiences in Teacher Education, Armidale.

Lowther, M. A. (1968). Most and Least Helpful Activities of Supervising Teachers. *Clearing House* 43: 20-23.

Mahajan, J. (1992). A Comparative Study of the Effectiveness of Two Models of Teaching *viz.* Bruner's Concept Attainment Model and Ausubel's Advance Organizer Model on Teaching Abilities of Student-Teachers and on Achievement of Students in Various Schools. Ph.D., Educ., Shreemati Nathibai Damodar Thackersey Women's Univ. Bombay.

Maheshwari, V. (1976). A Study Into the Classroom Verbal Interaction Pattern of Effective and Ineffective Teachers. Ph.D. Edu. Meerut Univ. Meerut.

Malhara, S. B. (1988). A Comparative Study of the Relative Effectiveness of the Teaching Methods Based on Motivation due to Competition and Motivation due to Initiative Spirit, Interest and Tendency to Co-operate. Independent Study. Govt. Junior College of Ed., Jalgaon.

Mathew, R. (1980). Factorial Structure of Teaching Competencies Among Secondary School Teachers. Ph.D. Edu. M.S. Univ. Baroda.

MacKinnon, A.M., and Grunau, H. (1991). "Teacher Development Through Reflection, Community, and Discourse." Paper Presented at the Annual Meeting of the American Educational Research Association, Chicago.

MacLeoad G.R. (1981). Experimental Studies of the Outcomes of Microteaching. *South Pac. J. Teach. Educ.* 9: 31-42.

Marrou, J. R. (1989). The University Supervisor: A New Role in a Changing Workplace. *Teacher Educator*, 24(3), 13-19.

Martin, S. (1994). The Mentoring Process in Preservice Teacher Education. *School Organization*, 14, 269-277.

Mayer, R., & Goldberry, L. (1993). Searching for Reflection in the Student Teaching Experience: Two Case Studies. *Teacher Education Quarterly*, 20 (1), 13-27.

Maynard, T., & Furlong, J. (1993). Learning to Teach and Models of Mentoring. In D. McIntyre, H. Hagger, & M. Wilkin (Eds.),

Mentoring : Perspectives on School-Based Teacher Education (pp.69-85). Kogan Page. London.

McCulloch, M. (1979). School Experience on Initial B.Ed./B.Ed. Hons. Degree Validated by the Council for National Academic Awards (CNAA) London.

McCurdy, B. A. (1962). A Study of the Availability of Certain Basic Experiences Provided off Campus Student Teachers in Terms of Indicated Needs (Doctoral Thesis, School of Education, Indiana University, Bloomington) Dissertation Abstracts International 1963 23: 2807-808 (University Microfilms No. 12-5789).

McDonald, F. J. (1982). Study of Induction Programs for Beginning Teachers Executive Summary. Educational Testing Services, Princeton, New Jersey.

McGreal, T.L. (1983). Successful Teacher Evaluation. VA : Association for Supervision and Curriculum Development Alexandria.

McIntyre, D.J., & Morris, W. R. (1980). Research on the Student Teaching Triad. *Contemporary Education*, 51(4), 193-196.

McIntyre, D. J. (1 984). A Response to Critics of Field Experience Supervision . *Journal of Teacher Education*, 35(3), 42-45.

McNally, P., & Martin, S. (1997). Support and Challenge in Learning to Teach: The Role of the Mentor. Manuscript in Preparation.

McNay, M., and Cole, A.L. (1993). "A Whole School Approach to the Practicum." *McGill Journal of Education*, 28(1), 115-131.

Medical Council of India (1983). Recommendations on Graduate Medical Education. Published and Sold by The Medical Council of India.

Medley, D.M. and Mitzel, H.E., (1963a). 'The Scientific Study of Teacher Behaviour.' In Bellack, A.A. (ed.) *Theory and Research in Teaching*, Teachers College Press, Columbia Univ. New York.

Medlye, D.M. and Mitzel, H.E. (1963b). *Measuring, Classroom Behaviour by Systematic Observation.* Rand Mc Nally, Chicago.

Mehta, S.J. (1973). An Investigation into the Effectiveness of Programmed Material in English for Developing Reading Ability Ph.D. Edu. M.S. Univ. Baroda.

Merseth, K. K. (1991). The Case for Cases in Teacher Education. Washington, D. C.: American Association of Colleges for Teacher Education/American Association of Higher Education.

M.H.R.D. Govt. of India (1986). *National Policy on Education.* New Delhi.

M.H.R.D. Govt. of India (1986). *Programme of Action.* New Delhi.

M.H.R.D. Govt. of India (1992). *Programme of Action.* New Delhi.

Mishra, P. K. (1985). A Comparative Study of Different Feedback Methods for Changing Teacher Behaviour. Ph.D. Psy. Utkal Univ. Bubane shwar.

Mohanty, S.B. (1984). A Study of Student Teaching Programmes in Colleges of Education with Special Reference to Innovation, Ph.D. Edu. M.S. Univ. Baroda.

More, R. T. (1988). A Study of Relationship Between Personality, Aptitude for Teaching and Effectiveness of Secondary Teachers. Ph.D., Edu. Nagpur Univ.

Mukhopadhyay, M. *et al.* (1981). An Action Research on Alternative Models of Teacher Training, TTTI, Bhopal.

Morris J. R. (1974). The Effects of the University Supervisor on the Performance and Adjustment of Student Teachers. *J. Educ. Res.* 67: 358-62.

Naik, V. V. (1984). A Comparative Study of the Effect of Microteaching and Conventional Approaches of Teacher Training Upon Pupils' Achievement, Pupils' Perception and General Teaching Competence of Preservice Student Teachers. Ph.D. Edu. Bombay Univ. Bombay.

Natrajan, S.A., (1984). A Competency Based Programme in Teacher Education Curriculum. Ph.D. Edu., Madras Univ. Madras.

Nautiyal, A. K. (1992). The Efficiency of Teacher Performance as Related to Their Values, Effectiveness, Morale and Students Pervceived Teacher Characteristics. Ph.D., Edu. Hemvati Nandan Bahuguna, Garhwal Univ.

N.C.E.R.T. (1963). *Plan and Programme*. NCERT, New Delhi.

N.C.E.R.T. (1964). *Internship in Teaching*, N.C.E.R.T., New Delhi.

N.C.E.R.T. (1978). *Teacher Education Curriculum: A Framework.* NCERT, New Delhi.

N.C.E.R.T. (1979). *Organisation of Core Training Programme Package*. N.C.E.R.T. New Delhi.

N.C.E.R.T. (1988). National Curriculum for Teacher Education , Deptt. of Teacher Ed., Special Ed. and Ext. Services NCERT, New Delhi.

N.C.E.R.T. (1991). *Secondary Teacher Education Curriculum: Guidelines and Syllabi*. NCERT, New Delhi.

N.C.T.E. (1998). *Curriculum Framework of Quality Teacher Education.* NCTE, New Delhi.

Nias, J. (1976). School-Supervised Practice in Junior Schools. *Trends in Educ.* 1:23-27.

Nias, J. (1977). What Should Nellie do? Student Role Expectations for Head and Class Teachers on School-Supervised Practice. *Br.J. Teach. Educ.* 3 : 121-30.

Nicklas, M. S. (1960). A Comparative Study of Critical Incidents to Determine Recommended Techniques for Supervisors of Student Teachers (Doctoral Dissertation. University of Arkansas) Dissertation Abstracts International. 1960. 20: 4342.

Nicoll V. (1975). The Effects of Practice Teaching Upon the Anxiety Levels, Educational Attitudes and Teaching Behaviours of Student Teachers. BA Hons Thesis, University of Sydeney. Sydney.

Oak, A.W., (1986). A Critical Study of Microteaching Techniques with a View to Suggest Improvement in its Implementation in Colleges of Education. Deptt. of P.G. Edu. and Res., SNDT. Univ. Bombay.

Paikaray, G.S. (1981). A Comparison of Different Types of Feedback in Microteaching Upon Teaching Cornpetence and Attitude Towards Teaching of Student-Teachers. Ph.D. Edu., Utkal Univ. Bhubaneshwar.

Pandey, S.M. (1980). A Critical Study of Supervision Practices Ph.D. Edu. Avadh Univ. Faizabad.

Pandey, S. N. (1986). Effectiveness of Advance Organizer and Inquiry Training Models for Teaching Social Studies to Class VIII Students. Ph.D.Edu. B.H.U. Varanasi.

Pangotra, N.N. (1972). A Study of the Effects of Feedback from Different Sources on the Classroom Behaviour of Student Teachers Using the Techniques of Interaction Analysis, Ph.D. Edn., M.S. Univ. Baroda.

Pareck U. and Rao, T. V. (1971). Motivation Training of Mental Health (A Study of Teacher Behaviour and Student Mental Health). National Institute of Health Administration and Education, New Delhi.

Passi, B.K. and Sharma, S.K. (1982). A Study of Teaching Competency of Secondary School Teachers. Deptt. of Edu., Indore Univ.

Passi, B.K., and Sansanwal, D.N. (1991). Research in Teaching: A Trend Report. M.B. Buch (ed.) Fourth Survey of Research in Education N.C.E.R.T. New Delhi.

Passi, B.K., Singh, L.C., and Sansanwal, D.N. (1986). Implementing Training Strategies and Studying Effectiveness of Different Variations in Components of Training Strategy for Concept Attainment Model / Inquiry Training Model in Terms of Understanding, Competency, Reactions and Willingness of Student Teachers. Deptt. of Edu. DAVV, Indore.

Passi, B. K., Singh, L. C., and Sanswnwal, D. N. (1991). Models of Teaching: Report of the Three Phased Study of CAM and ITM. Independent Study. NCERT, New Delhi.

Patel, I.U. (1 975). A Comparative Study of Patterns of University Education in UK, USA, and USSR with Special Reference to the University Education in India Ph.D. Edu. Sardar Patel Univ.

Patel, P.A. (1978a). A Comparative Study of the Effects of Perceptual Modelling and Symbolic Modelling in Microteaching Under Simulated Conditions on General Teaching Competence and Attitude Towards Teaching of Student-Teachers. R.P. Anada College of Education, Borsad.

Patel, P.A. (1978b). A Study of the Relative Effectiveness of Microteaching and Traditional Technique of the Teacher Training in the Development of General Teaching Competence of the Student-Teachers of Primary Teachers Training College, R.P. Anada College of Education, Borsad.

Peters, W. H. (1971). An Investigation of the Influence of Cooperating Teachers in Shaping the Attitudes of Student Teachers Towards the Teaching of English. University of Kentucky, ERIC Document No. ED 074 052.

Phillips, L. L. (1977). Mentors and Proteges : A Study of the Career Development of Women Managers and Executives in Business and Industry. Unpublished Doctoral Dissertation, University of California at Los Angeles.

Poole, C. (1972). The Influence of Experiences in the Schools on Students' Evaluation of Teaching Practice. *J. Educ. Res.* 66: 161-64.

Poole, C., Gaudry E. (1974). Some Effects of Teaching Practice. *Aust. J. Educ.* 18(3): 255-63.

Pribram, K. H. (1986). The Cognitive Revolution and Mind/Brain Issues. *American Psychologist*, 41, 507-520.

Price, R. D. (1961). The Influence of Supervising Teachers. *J. Teach. Educ.* 12: 471-75.

Raina, V. K. (1995). Teacher Education in India : In Search of an Identity. *Jr. Teacher Education.* Vol.46. No. 1.

Ralph, E. (1991). Aboriginal Student-Teachers in the Extended Practicum: Contextual Supervision. *Teaching Education,* 4(1), 113-121.

Ralph, E. (1992). Continuous Teacher Development: A Case for Contextual Supervision. *Brock Education,* 2(3), 13-17.

Ralph, E. (1992-1993). Improving Practicum Supervision : A Canadian Experience. *Action in Teacher Education*, 14(4), 30-38.

Ralph, E. (1993a). Enhancing Aboriginal Teacher Education : One Promising Approach. *Canadian Journal of Native Education,* 20(1), 44-62.

Ralph, E. (1993b). Sensitive, Sensitive Practicum Supervision: A Contextual Application in Sakatchewan. *The Alberta Journal of Educational Research,* 39, 283-296.

Ralph, Edwin G. (1994). Helping Beginning Teachers Improve Via Contextual Supervision. *Jr. Teacher Edu.* Vol.45 . No. 5.

Raymond A. (1973). The Acquisition of Non-verbal Behaviours by Preservice Science Teachers and Their Application During Student Teaching. *J. Res. Sci. Teach.* 10: 13-24.

Ray, P.K.S. (1978). Effect of Various Treatments on the Acquisition of Teaching Skills Through Microteaching Ph.D. Edu., M.S. Univ. Baroda.

R.C.E. (1982). *Manual for Teacher Trainee and Supervisors,* R.C.E. Bhopal.

Reddy, N.Y. (1975). Programmed Learning *vs.* Conventional Learning in the Instruction of Language: A Comparative Study. Deptt. of Education, Osm. Univ.

R.I.E. (1995). Supervisor's Diary, Guideline or Internship Programme , Internship Supervision, Internship in Teaching (Micro Teaching), Lesson Observation Schedule, Lesson Notes, Supervision Notebook. R.I.E. Bhopal.

Rikard, G. L., & Knight, S.M. (1997). Obstacles to Professional Development: Interns' Desire to fit in, get Along, and be Real Teachers. *Journal of Teaching in Physical Education.* 16(4), 440-453.

Risk, Thomas M. (1965). Principles and Practices of Teaching in Secondary Schools. Eurasia Publishing House (Pvt.) Ltd. Ram Nagar, New Delhi.

Ronnestad, M. H., & Skoyholt, T. M, (1993). Supervision of Beginning and Advanced Graduate Students of Counselling and Psychotherapy. *Journal of Counselling and Development,* 71, 396-405.

Rosenshine, Barak (1995). Advances in Research on Instruction. *Jr. Educ. Res.* Vol.88 No.5.

Rothman, L. S. (1981). Effective and Ineffective Supervisory Behaviour of College Supervisors as Perceived by Secondary School Cooperating Teachers (Doctoral Dissertation, The University of Florida). *Dissertation Abstracts International,* 42(5), 2086A.

Rovegno, I. (1992). Learning to Teaching in a Field-Based Methods Course: The Development of Pedagogical Content Knowledge. *Teaching and Teacher Education,* 8, 69-82.

Russell, T., and Munby, H. (eds.) (1992). *Teachers and Teaching : From Classroom to Reflection.* Falmer Press. Washington, D.C.

Ryans, D.G. (1960). *Characteristics of Teachers. American Council of Teaching.* Washington D.C.

Ryan, K. (1982). The Cooperating Teacher: Who? Why? When? How? And Whither? In G. Griffin & S. Edwards (Eds.). *Student Teaching: Problems and Promising Practices.* Preceding of a Working Conference (pp. 57-68). Research and Development Center for Teacher Education. Austin, TX.

Saunders, S., Pettinger, K., & Tomlinson, P. (1995). Prospective Mentors' Views on Partnership in Secondary Teacher Training. *British Educational Research Journal,* 21(2), 199-218.

Schon, D. (1987). *Educating the Reflective Practitioner.* Jossey-Bass. San Francisco.

Sergiovanni, T. (1992). *Moral Leadership: Getting to the Heart of School Improvement.* Jossey-Bass, San Francisco.

Shah, B. (1991). Determinanats of Teacher Effectiveness Independent Study. Rohilkhand Univ.

Shah, M. M. (1986). A Survey of Management of Student Teaching in India. CASE, M.S. Univ. Baroda.

Shaida, A.K. (1976). Teaching Pattern—Questioning, Feedback, and Pupil Attainment, Ph.D. Edu, M.S. Univ. Baroda.

Sharma, A.K. (1986). Effect of Different Microteaching Settings on the Development of Probing Questioning Skill and Verbal Classroom Interaction. Ph.D. Edu. Meerut Univ. Meerut.

Sharma, K.K. (1977). Effect of Different Techniques of Feedback Upon the Attainment of Teaching Skills Related to Stimulus Variations Among Teachers, Ph.D. Edu. M.S. Univ., Baroda.

Sharma, R. A. (1971). A Study of the Relationship of Predictors of Teacher Effectiveness of Elementary Level and Follow up After one Year of Training, D. Phil, Edu. Meerut Univ. Meerut.

Sharma, S. (1972). Relationship Between Patterns of Teacher Classroom Behaviour and Pupils' Attainment in Terms of Instructional Objectives, Ph.D. Edu. M.S. Univ. Baroda.

Sharma, Y.K. and Kumar, N. (1983). Relative Importance of Teaching Skills: Views of Secondary School Teachers. *Jr. Ind. Ed.* Vol. 8, No.6.

Shipman, M. D. (1967). Theory and Practice in the Education of Teachers. *Educational Researcher,* 9(3), 208-212.

Shukla, S. (1981). Identification of Major Skills Involved in Mathematics Teaching at Secondary School Stage. Ph. D. Edu. B.H. Univ. (B.H.U.). Varanasi.

Shulman, J. H., and Colbert, J. A. (eds.) (1988). The Intern Teacher Casebook: Cases and Commentaries. San Francisco: Far West Laboratory for Educational Research and Development.

Sidhu, P.S. (1983). A Follow-up Study of Secondary School Teachers Trained Through Different Approaches Ph.D. Edu. D.A.V.V. Indore.

Silverman, R., Welty, W.M., and Lyon, S. (1991). *Case Studies for Teacher Problem-Solving.* McGraw-Hill. New York.

Sinclair, K, Nicoll, V. (1981). Sources and Experience of Anxiety in Practice Teaching. *South Pacific J. Teach. Educ.* 9: 1-18.

Singh, G. (1982). Comparative Study Different Strategies of Integration of Teaching Skills, Ph.D. Edu. B.H. Univ. (B.H.U). Varanasi.

Singh. L.C. (1982). *Third National Survey of Secondary Teacher Education in India*, NCERT, New Delhi.

Singh, L.P. (1974). Interaction Analysis, Microteaching and Modification of Teacher Classroom Behaviour, Ph.D. Edu. M.S. Univ. Baroda.

Singh, N. (1985). A Comparative Study of Teachers Trained Through Integrated and Traditional Methods in Terms of Attitude Towards Teaching, Teaching Competence and Role Performance, Ph.D. Edu, B.H. Univ. (B.H.U.). Varanasi.

Singh, O. (1983). Effects of Mastery Learning Strategies on Certain Non-Cognitive Variables of High School Students. Ph.D.Edu. HPU. Simla.

Singh, Satynarayan (1984). Effect of Training in Teaching Skills Using Micro-Class, Peers and Real Pupils on the General Teaching Competence of Student Teachers. DSERT, Karnataka.

Singh, S. K. (1987). A Study of the Effect of Remedial Instructional Microteaching Course on Instructional Competence of In-service Primary School Science-Teachers. Ph.D. Edu. Karnatak Univ.

Singh, S. K. (1988). A Study of Relationship Between Verbal Interaction of Teachers in Class and Attitude Towards Teaching. Ph.D. Edu. Univ. of Gorakhpur.

Singh, T. (1988). A Study of Teaching Efficiency in Relation to Job Satisfaction and Socio-Economic Status of Secondary School Teachers. Ph.D., Edu. Avadh. Univ.

Smith, B. O. (1980). *A Design for a School of Pedagogy*. U.S. Government Printing Office. Washington, D. C.

Smith, B.O., Cohen, S. B., and Pearl, A. (1969). *Teachers for the*

Real World. American Association of Colleges of Teacher Education. Washington, D. C.

Smyth, J. W. (1986). An Alternative and Critical Perspective for Clinical Supervision in Schools in K. Sirotnik & J. Oakes (Eds.), *Critical Perspectives on the Organization and Improvement of Schooling* (pp. 131-161). Kluwer-Nijhoff. Boston.

Sonthall, C., & King, D. F. (1979). Critical Incidents in Student Teaching. *Teacher Educator*, 15(2), 34-36.

Sperling, G. (1960). The Information Available in Brief Visual Presentations. *Psychological Monograph*, 74 (Whole No. 498).

Sperry, R. W. (1993). The Impact and Promise of the Cognitive Revolution. *American Psychologist*, 48, 878-885.

Spiro, R.J., *et al.* (1987). Knowledge Acquisition for Application: Cognitive Flexibility and Transfer in Complex Domains. In B.C. Britton (ed.), *Executive Control Processes*. Erlbaum. Hills-dale, N.J.

Stallings, J. A., Bossung, J., and Martin, A. (1990). Houston Teaching Academy: Partnership in Developing Teachers. *Teaching and Teacher Education*, 6, 355-365.

Stallings, J. A., and Kowalski, T. J. (1990). Research on Professional Development Schools. In W.R.Houston (ed.), *Handbook of Research on Teacher Education*. Macmillan. New York.

Stallings, J. (1991). Connecting Pre-service Teacher Education and In-service Professional Development: A Professional Development School. Paper Presented at the Annual Meeting of the American Educational Research Association, Chicago.

Stapleton M. C. (1965). An Evaluation of two Programmes of Student Teacher Supervision by College Supervisors. Doctoral Dissertation, Pennsylvania State University, University Park, Pennsylvania.

State of Vermont (1993). Licensing Standards for Vermont Educators. State Department of Education. Montpelier, VT.

Stewig, J. W. (1970). What Should College Supervisors do? *J. Teach Educ.* 21:251-57.

Stenberg, R. J. (1977). *Intelligence, Information Processing and Analogical Reasoning : The Componential Analysis of Human Abilities*. Lawrence Erlbaum. Hillsdale, NJ.

Stones, E. & Morris, S. (1972). *Teaching Practice : Problems and Perspectives*. Methuen & Co. Ltd. London.

Strang, H. R., Landrum, M. S., and Lynch, K. A. (1989). Talking with the Computer: A Simulation for Training Basic Teaching Skills. *Teaching and Teacher Education*, 5, 143-153.

Strawderman, C., and Lindsey, P. (1995) . Keeping up with the Times: Reform in Teacher Education. *Jr. Teacher Edu.* Vol.46, No.2.

Sultana, A. (1988). A Study of Modification of Behaviour of Pupil-Teachers of Science Through Microteachng Approach with Special Reference to Gorakhpur University. Ph.D., Edu. Univ. of Gorakhpur.

Sushma, (1987). Effectiveness of Concept Attainment and Biological Science Inquiry Models of Teaching Biological Science to VIII Class Students. Ph.D. Educ. B.H.U. Varanasi.

Swamy, Narsimha, N.(1984). Diagnosis and Remediation of Deficiencies in Basic Understanding of Prospective Teachers of Secondary School. Ph.D. Edu. Mysore Univ. Mysore.

Switzer, R. (1976). Co-operating Teachers : Strengths and Weaknesses. *Colorado J. Educ. Res.* 15(2): 37-45.

Syag, R.N. (1984). Study of Teaching Competence of Pre-service and In-service Teachers Trained Through Different Treatments of Microteaching. Ph.D. Edu. D.A.V.V. Indore.

Sykes, G., and Bird, T. (1992). Teacher Education and the Case Idea. In G.E. Grant (ed.), *Review of Research in Education*, Vol. 18. American Educational Research Association. Washington, D.C.

Taba, H. (1965). *Teaching Strategies and Cognitive Functioning in Elementary School Children*. San Francisco State College. San Francisco.

Tabachnick, B.R., and Zeichner, K.M. (1984). The Impact of the Student Teaching Experience on the Development of Teacher Perspectives. *Journal of Teacher Education,* 35(6), 28-36.

Tannehill, D. (1989). Student Teaching : A View from the Other Side. *Journal of Teaching in Physical Education*, 8, 243-253.

Tannehill, D., & Zakrajsek, D. (1988). What's Happening in Supervision of Student Teachers in Secondary Physical Education ? *Journal of Teaching in Physical Education,* 8(1), 1-12.

Taylor J. K. Dale I. R. (1971). *A Survey of Teachers in Their First Year of Service.* University of Bristol School of Education. Bristol.

Teprongtong, S. (1984). Role Expectations and the Role Performance of College Supervisors on Student Teaching as Perceived by School Principals, Cooperating Teachers and Student Teachers Ph.D. Edu., Pan. Univ.

Thakur, T. (1976). *Who is a Good teacher* ? (A Study Based on the Opinion of Senior Pupils). SIE Assam.

Tisher R. (ed.) (1978). *The Induction of Beginning Teachers in Australia.* School of Education Monash University. Melbourne.

Tisher R. (1980). The Induction of Beginning Teachers. In : Hoyle E, Megarry L (eds.) *World Yearbook of Education 1980: Professional Development of Teachers,* Kogan Page London.

Tisher, R. P. (1995). Readjustments, Reorganisation or Revolution? The Changing Face of Teacher Education in Australia. In M. F. Wideen & P.P. Grimmett (Eds.), *Changing Times in Teacher Education* (pp. 34-46). Falmer. Bristol, PA.

Tomlinson, P. (1995). *Understanding Mentoring : Reflective Strategies for School-Based Teacher Preparation.* Open University Press. Milton Keynes, UK.

Trimmer, R. L. (1961). Tell us More, *Student Teacher. J. Teach. Educ.* 1 2: 228-31.

Tuckman, B. W., Oliver, W. F. (1968). Effectiveness of Feedback to Teachers as a Function of Source. *J. Educ. Psychol.* 59 : 297-301

Tulley, Michael & Chiu, Lian Hawang (1995). Student Teachers and Classroom Discipline. *Jr. Educ. Res.* Vol.88, No.3.

Tulving, E., Mandler, G.Y., & Baumel, R. (1964). Interaction of two Sources of Information in Tachistoscopic Word Recognition. *Canadian Journal of Psychol.*, 18, 62-71.

Turner, M. (1993). The Role of Mentors and Teacher Tutors in School-based Teacher Education and Induction. *British Journal of In-Service Education*, 19, 36-45.

Turney C, Clift J. C, Dunking M. J., Traill R. D. (1973). Microteaching : Research, Theory and Practice : An Innovation in Teacher Education especially as it Relates to the Australian Context. Sydney University Press, Sydney.

Turney, C. *et al.* (1982). *Supervisor Development Programmnes.* Sydney Univ. Press, Sydney.

Vasishtha, K.K. (1976). An Experimental Study of the Change in Some Characteristics and Verbal Behaviour of Secondary Science and Mathematics Student-Teachers Through Training in Verbal Interaction Technique. Ph.D. Edu. Meerut. Univ. Meerut.

Vaze, N .A., (1976). Effects of Modelling and Microteaching of the Acquisition of Certain Skills in Questioning, Ph.D. Edu., M.S. Univ. Baroda.

Veal, M. L., and Rikard, L. (1998). Cooperating Teachers' Perspectives on the Student Teaching Triad. *J. Teacher Ed.* Vol.49, No.2.

Wager, A. C. (1973). Changing Teacher Behavior : A Comparison of Microteaching and Cognitive Discrimination Training. *Journal of Educational Psychology*, 64, 299-305.

Wallas, G. (1926). *The Art of Thought.* Harcourt Brace, New York.

Watkins, O. C., & Watkins, M. J. (1980). The Modality Effect and Echoic Persistence. *Journal of Experimental Psychology : General*, 109, 251-278.

Watzlawick, P. (1978). *The Language of Change*. New York : Basic Books.

Welborn, E. L. (1920). Cooperation with Local Schools in Student Teaching. *Educational Administration and Supervision*, 6, 445-470.

Wheatley, M. (1994). Leadership and the New Science: Learning About Organizations from an Orderly Universe. Berrett-Koehler, Inc. San Francisco.

Winitski, N., Stoddard, T., & O'Keefe, P. (1992). Great Expectations: Emergent Professional Development Schools. *Journal of Teacher Education*, 43, 3-18.

Wiseman, S., Start, K. B. (1965). A Follow up of Teachers Five years After Their Training. *Brit. J. Educ. Psychol.* 35: 242-61.

Wildman, T. M, Magliero, S. G., Niles, R. A., & Niles, J. A. (1992). Teacher Mentoring : An Analysis of Roles, Activities, and Conditions. *Journal of Teacher Education*, 43, 205-213.

Wilkin, M. (1992). On the Cusp: From Supervision to Mentoring in Initial Teacher Training. *Cambridge Journal of Education*, 22(1), 79-90.

Woods, P. (1987). "Life Histories and Teacher Knowledge." In J.Smyth (ed.), *Educating Teachers: Changing the Nature of Pedagogical Knowledge*. Falmer Press. Washington, D.C.

World Bank (1997). *Primary Education in India*. Allied Publishers Ltd. New Delhi.

Wragg E. (1970). Interaction Analysis as a Feedback System for Student '*Teachers. Educ. Teach.* 81: 38-47.

Yadav, R.A. (1983). A Study of the Effect of Training for Classroom Questioning Behaviour on Teaching Competence and Pupil Achievement. Ph.D. Edu. Meerut. Univ. Meerut.

Yee, A. H. (1968). Interpersonal Relationships in the Student Teaching Triad. *Journal of Teacher Education*, 19, 95-112.

Yee, A. H. (1969). Do Co-operating Teachers Influence the Attitudes of Student Teacher ? *J. Educ. Psychol.* 60: 327-32.

Zeichner, K. M., and Liston, D.P. (1987). "Teaching Student Teachers to Reflect." *Harvard Educational Review*, 57(1), 23-48.

Zeichner, K. M. (1987). "The Ecology of Field Experience: Towards Understanding the Role of Field Experiences." In M. Haberman and J.M. Backus (eds.), *Advances in Teacher Education,* Vol.3. Ablex. Norwood, NJ.

Zeichner K. M. (1979). Teacher Induction Practices in the United States and Great Britain. University of Wisconsin, Department of Curriculum and Instruction, Madison, Wisconsin.

Zeichner, K. M., Teitelbaum, K. (1982). Personalized and Inquiry Oriented Teacher Education : An Analysis of two Approaches to the Development of Curriculum for Field Based Experience. *J. Educ. Teaching,* 8(2).

Zimpher, N., de Voss, G., & Nott, D. (1980). A Closer Look at University Student Teacher Supervision. *Journal of Teacher Education*, 31(4), 11-15.

Zulich, J., Bean, T. W., and Herrick, J. (1991). Charting Stages of Pre-service Teacher Development and Reflection in a Multicultural Community Through Dialogue Journal Analysis. Paper Presented at the Annual Meeting of the American Educational Research Association, Chicago.

Zumwalt, K. K. (1982). "Research on Teaching: Policy Implications for Teacher Education." In A. Lieberman and M. W. McLaughlin (eds.), *Policy Making in Education.* (81 st Yearbook of the National Society for the Study of Education, Part 1). University of Chicago Press. Chicago.

INDEX